Imperialism and War

Walter L. Hixson since 2019 serves as columnist and contributing editor at the *Washington Report on Middle East Affairs*. His two recent books on the Israel lobby are *Architects of Repression: How Israel and its Lobby Put Racism, Violence and Injustice at the Center of US Middle East Policy* (Institute for Research, 2021) and *Israel's Armor: The Israel Lobby and the First Generation of the Palestine Conflict.* (Cambridge University Press, 2019) He is the author of several books focused on the history of US foreign relations, including *American Foreign Relations: A New Diplomatic History* (Routledge, 2015), *American Settler Colonialism: A History* (2013, Palgrave-Macmillan), *The Myth of American Diplomacy: National Identity and U.S. Foreign Policy* (Yale University Press, 2008). More at www.WalterHixson.com.

Imperialism and War:

The History Americans Need to Own

By Walter L. Hixson

Copyright © 2021 Institute for Research
All rights reserved.
Library of Congress Cataloging-in-Publication Data

Names: Hixson, Walter L., author.
Title: Imperialism and war : the history Americans need to own /
by Walter L. Hixson.
Identifiers: LCCN 2021030800 (print) |
LCCN 2021030801 (ebook) |
ISBN 9780982775790 (hardcover) ISBN 9780982775752 (paperback) |
ISBN 9780982775769 (kindle edition)
Subjects: LCSH: United States--Foreign relations. |
United States—Military policy. | Imperialism. | Exceptionalism--United
States. | Nationalism--United States--History. | United
States--History--Philosophy.
Classification: LCC E183.7 .H5944 2021 (print) | LCC E183.7
(ebook) | DDC 325/.320973--dc23
LC record available at https://lccn.loc.gov/2021030800
LC ebook record available at https://lccn.loc.gov/2021030801

Contents

Introduction

The history of American foreign relations, like American history in general, is shrouded in mythology. Millions of Americans embrace a nationalist discourse that depicts the United States as a "beacon of liberty," the "world's best hope," the leader of the "free world."

The faith in "American exceptionalism" has propelled myriad national achievements as well as the rise to global preeminence, but there is also a dark side to this history. National self-worship has enabled the nation's history of continental and overseas aggression, which is the subject of this book. Patriotic sentiment depicting the United States as "a global force for good," as the onetime Navy recruitment campaign asserted, has worked to enable and to justify perennial campaigns of imperialism and war. In an irony that is little explored yet permeates American history, benevolent discourse has long provided a foundation for violent aggression.

This book argues that it is long past time to unpack this destructive discourse animated by national self-worship and to replace it with a desperately needed new paradigm of cooperative internationalism. Carrying out such a transition is the only actual "last best hope" if we are to have any chance of addressing the profound challenges of the present day and of the global future.

The Sweep of American History

In the late eighteenth century, as they launched a revolt against monarchy and aristocracy--an uprising that reverberated across the globe--Americans proudly proclaimed that their nation was the global exemplar of human freedom and progress. Strongly and often fervently religious in the aftermath of the "Great Awakening" revival that had swept across the continent, masses of Americans came to believe that the United States was a "chosen" nation, providentially destined to lead the world.

The potent patriotic discourse of American exceptionalism provided the glue that forged the unlikely and fragile union of 13 highly disparate British colonies stretching from New Hampshire to Georgia. Patriotic nationalism spurred a strong sense of "can-do" optimism within the newly imagined community. The United States became a magnet for immigrants, which helped fuel economic growth and the eventual rise to global power. At the same time, however, American hubris functioned as a curse, one

1

that fueled the nation's penchant for identifying supposedly inferior enemy others and subjecting them to aggression and war.

As a critical mass of people repeatedly affirmed the concept of the nation's destiny and greatness, that discourse became hegemonic and enduring. This ritualized invocation of American exceptionalism, passed down from generation to generation, made it real to people. America was the "land of the free" and thus it followed that its foreign policy must advance the cause of freedom and democracy. These were simply words, but they were said and otherwise represented so ubiquitously—in poetry, in song, in the waving of the flag--that they became reified as if they were truth and became inculcated into national culture.

The United States did, as "beacon of liberty" discourse would have it, sometimes inspire and help other peoples to pursue freedom and democracy. More often, however, as this book will show, the United States acted as a militant and imperial power. Thus, to a considerable extent--one far greater than national mythology is inclined to acknowledge—the United States has carried out a deeply flawed and reactionary foreign policy. The consequences of these actions, both at home and abroad, have been profound and yet remain poorly understood.

"American" aggression began the day that Cristoforo Columbo inadvertently sailed into the Bahamas. The famed Admiral may have been hopelessly lost in 1492, but he came equipped with plenty of Eurocentric attitude, nonetheless. He quickly observed that the indigenous islanders that he encountered were well built, ignorant and heathen peoples who would make good "servants."

Columbus and his followers proceeded to unleash centuries of enslavement and removal policies targeting indigenous people. The European interlopers laid the foundation of white supremacy, war, and imperialism that the ebullient Americans inherited three centuries later and instilled into their own national identity.

After the Revolution, the new United States was a progressive nation for elite white men only. It remained a brutally repressive regime for the non-white peoples who were variously enslaved and driven from their homelands. *Centuries* of ethnic cleansing of indigenous people as well as *centuries* of mass enslavement of African Americans left an indelible imprint on national identity. The inspired discourse of republicanism in the Declaration of Independence and the US Constitution allowed for amelioration but could not transcend the deep-seated cultural identity.

This book homes in on the interplay between American national identity and a foreign policy characterized by imperialism and war. While many books focus on US military history—it is a difficult subject to ignore, as Americans have almost always been at war with someone--relatively few have the temerity to include imperialism, or its cousin colonialism in their titles or interpretive frameworks on American history. War and imperialism permeate American history, yet because historical discourse is disciplined by the norms of patriotic nationalism they have been poorly analyzed in many American *histories*, professional as well as popular.

The basic definition of imperialism is the extension of a nation's power and influence over another people through a range of tactics from direct intervention to diplomacy. Imperialism, however, has been a loaded term. After all, *communists* associated imperialism with the capitalist West and that alone has been enough to preclude mainstream application of the term to the United States. Although Marxist theorists emphasized materialist motivations, imperialism is sometimes pursued for non-economic motives such as national prestige or perceived security aims.

The essence of imperialism is the imposition of power at the expense and without the consent of the people subjected to it. Often accompanied in history by racial, religious, and other forms of invidious comparison or demonization, imperialism entails the violation of the freedom and equality of one people by a self-interested and expanding other. Regardless of the motives and justifications, imperialism is a will to power, a denial of self-determination, an exploitative relationship typically backed by intimidation and violence.

Imperialism in traditional accounts of American history typically debuts as an aberration in the context of the so-called Spanish-American War of 1898. At that time some prominent Americans were upset enough about the US decision to seize control of non-contiguous lands on opposite sides of the world that they met in Boston and launched the Anti-Imperialist League in 1899. They lost the subsequent debate, however, as the American public largely embraced imperialism. Much of the American public recognized, as Theodore Roosevelt and others argued at the time, that subjugating people perceived as racially inferior was consistent with national identity. In other words, the United States had always been an imperialistic nation, which until that time had been engaged primarily in driving indigenous people from their homelands. The United States was thus, as Roosevelt insisted, "making no new departure" in dominating other peoples and taking over foreign lands.

To be sure, not all individual Americans were then, nor are now, war-mongering imperialists. All Americans nonetheless did then, and do now, live within an imperial culture. The millions of Americans who have opposed US wars and imperialism over the generations, like the *fin de siècle* anti-imperialists, have fought a mostly losing battle because they have run headlong into the militant nationalism that flows from American exceptionalism. Thus, throughout US history a critical mass of Americans has either supported imperialism and war or been insufficiently dedicated or empowered to do anything about them.

3

Wars have been waged continuously throughout the broad sweep of American pre-history and history. American settler colonialism—the uprooting, removing, and killing of the indigenous people of North America—was an imperial project. Driving Indians from the land was the necessary precondition for the creation of the American colonies that eventually became the United States. The centuries of ethnic cleansing of a putatively inferior and "savage" people left a deep imprint on American identity and on foreign policy.

Owing to the self-worship that is intrinsic to national identity, few studies even by professional historians emphasize or try to grapple with the fundamental historical continuity between continental aggression and the subsequent and similarly aggressive US global foreign policy that followed. While the significance of the "frontier" on American history has long and even famously been acknowledged, it remains misunderstood and under-appreciated. Western expansion was a sixteenth-, seventeenth- and eighteenth-century and not merely the nineteenth-century phenomenon propagated by the vintage Hollywood Westerns. Ditto with the "Old South." This study thus reconnects the much longer history of frontier aggression with the subsequent era of overseas war and imperialism that it spawned.

The scholars and journalists who have criticized American militarism have focused overwhelmingly on the post-World War II period. Criticism of military disasters in Vietnam, Iraq and Afghanistan thus has remained largely disconnected from the centuries of continental ethnic cleansing that preceded those conflicts. But the wars in Indochina and the Middle East were not aberrations, rather they were products of a continuous national identity and foreign policy deeply rooted in a long history of aggression and war.

By treating wars and intervention as aberrations, we fail to fully understand them. Critics of the more recent and failed bouts of militarism sometimes chide, "That's not who we are," which misses the main lesson to be learned, namely that it *is* who we are.

The imperial dis-connect between "frontier" and overseas empire works to affirm myths such as "manifest destiny." Under this celebratory Christian and white supremacist framework, the history of nineteenth century American Western expansion was not a history of war and imperialism but rather the inevitable, providentially sanctioned triumph of civilization over savagery. The "Winning of the West" was predestined, a Darwinian advance of modernity and progress--as opposed to a continent-wide ethnic cleansing that fueled a legacy of imperialism and war.

A related feature of nationalist mythology suggests that Americans have gone to war only reluctantly, typically because they "had to" to protect their "national security." The notion that the United States is

4

inclined toward "isolationism," or has gone to war reluctantly or only as a last resort, has long been a popular distortion of American history. The truth, as this book will show, is that the United States has been *choosing* imperialism and war throughout its history.

While Americans have claimed to wage wars to make the world "safe for democracy," the reality typically has diverged from the rhetoric. Wars were rarely fought for the purpose of promoting democracy nor did they usually achieve that result. The nation has frequently intervened, both covertly and overtly, to support authoritarian and even blatantly and brutally repressive regimes. Such regimes were perceived as better positioned to enhance the "national interest," which included ensuring access to natural resources and global markets while repressing left-wing or even merely reform-minded movements and democratically elected governments. The truth, as the book will conclusively demonstrate, is that the United States has often intervened *against* democracy.

Another important characteristic of American foreign policy and thus of this study is the propensity the United States has displayed through imperialism and war to create the conditions for blowback. As referenced in internal CIA documents, blowback alludes to the unintended and undesirable consequences that often resulted from US intervention. War and imperialism thus have consequences--often very bad ones--including sometimes achieving little more than laying the foundation for the next war. As this study will show, foreign interventions frequently backfired throughout American history, producing adverse results.

American wars and imperialism have been highly and often indiscriminately destructive--yet another marginalized aspect of the history of US foreign relations. Millions of people have been killed and wounded through American aggression, beginning with the continental ethnic cleansing project. While highly sensitive about incurring casualties of their own in warfare, Americans, it seems fair to say, have lost relatively little sleep over the massive destruction of other people and societies. As this book will show, the United States has also supported various allies as they slaughtered masses of people. American elites thus frequently decided that enabling mass murder abroad served the "national interest."

Superpower Status

By the mid-twentieth century the United States had become the preeminent global "superpower" and developed a "military-industrial complex" that was unprecedented in world history. In the post-World War II era, national security elites relentlessly pursued economic and foreign policies centered on securing unfettered access to natural resources located in other parts of the world. They would support virtually any foreign entity, no matter how repressive or authoritarian, in order to get these resources, especially petroleum. The United States invested heavily in preparing for and profiting from foreign intervention. Imperialism and war became institutionalized—and globalized. Empire, as the legendary diplomatic historian William A. Williams once put it, constituted an American "way of life."

American imperialism and warfare have had a deleterious effect on domestic life and society. This aspect, too, has received far too little attention. As the nation intervened abroad, often with disastrous consequences, it began at the same time to neglect and even disdain the ability to devise and implement thoughtful and effective domestic policies. The United States invested trillions of dollars and massive human energies in war and imperialism, resources that could have been devoted to improving and making more progressive and egalitarian its own society.

War and imperialism, as discussed in the pages that follow, also undermined civil liberties on the home front. Freedom of speech entailing criticism of foreign intervention has been unwelcomed and often punished in wartime. At all times the "national security state" safeguarded its turf by demonizing and sometimes jailing critics as unpatriotic.

The penchant for war and imperialism undermined the American left. In contrast with Western Europe, where an actual socialist leaning left provided balance and alternatives within domestic political debates, the United States stifled left-wing politics. The socialist leaning left was attacked beginning in the nineteenth century and then thoroughly delegitimized under the Cold War in the second half of the twentieth century. The purge and marginalization of the American left in the Cold War--though highly consequential--is yet another under-told and under-appreciated story within the dominant patriotic narrative of American history.

In US public discourse when news commentators or ordinary Americans say, "the left" what they actually mean is "liberal." US politics especially since World War II begin at the liberal center and flows from there to the right. Crucially absent in postwar American politics, though attempting to make a comeback at present, is the counterbalancing force of a genuine and viable left-wing. Militarism and imperialism thus complemented conservative and right-wing thought while closing off the cultural space required for progressive ideas to flourish.

National mythology continually reaffirms itself while at the same time enabling ongoing foreign policy militancy. The hegemonic discourse of American exceptionalism and its accompanying militancy work hand in hand as an organic, self-perpetuating cultural phenomenon. The nation thus celebrated the supposed victory in the Cold War, eliding the attendant mass violence, support for reactionary regimes, depletion of energy and resources, neglect of domestic needs, and erosion of civil liberties that the conflict entailed. Declaring "victory" in the Cold War put a positive spin on aggression and war, laying the foundation for the next wave of militarism. Today imperial discourse sanctions global intervention, including the "forever wars" and the targeted assassinations which are now an everyday feature of the self-perpetuating "global war on terror."

Despite many failed war efforts, the United States glorifies militarism--as well as domestic policing--and stoutly defends these outposts of militancy even when the criticism directed their way rests on firm ground. The ever-rising Pentagon budget is sacrosanct—US "defense" spending reaches record levels with each passing year while domestic programs compete for remaining funds, which typically have been squeezed in the wake of ever more tax cuts for the rich. The only social welfare programs you can be sure will be enacted with little criticism by Congress are those like the various GI bills that undergird military recruitment.

Foreign policy militancy ritualistically calls on Americans to "support our troops" by sending them off to be killed and maimed, psychologically if not physically. The focus on *our* troops at the same time obscures the impact of US militarism abroad. While US troops are celebrated as heroes, less attention has been focused on their use of the most lethal military technology in human history to kill and maim masses of "enemy" combatants, not to mention non-combatants, as is often the case. Also obscured amid the ritualistic worship of "our military heroes" are the stunningly high levels of violence and sexual assault that have emanated from military academies and overseas bases. The US military has long cultivated a star chamber style of military proceedings, which in practice meant that sexual violence long went unpoliced and unpunished. While soldiers are depicted as heroes, peace activists, human rights activists, and whistle blowers have been demonized in mainstream culture.

The United States is by no means the only militant and imperial nation in world history, though it is one of the most arrogant owing to the critical role that the discourse of exceptionalism plays in America's formally democratic society. The point of this book is not to demonize the United States, but rather to de-mythologize its history; to unpack the enabling hegemonic discourse; to critically analyze the sweep of US history and foreign policy; and to call attention to the devastating effects of imperial violence, both abroad and at home.

As war and imperialism are inherently destructive of life, and as human energies are better devoted to more beneficent pursuits--especially considering the existential challenges that confront humanity today--I come out against them here. A book like this, which calls on the United States to take ownership of its clear and verifiable historical transgressions, will be condemned by some as "revisionist history." This popular term of opprobrium ignores that historians are constantly engaged in revising the past based on new information and fresh perspectives. Revisionism is the very stuff of history.

All histories are inherently subjective and judgmental, however much they may adopt the trappings of mythical objectivity. Patriotically inclined history emphasizes America's supposed role as the providentially destined leader of the "free world" and thus celebrates assertions of righteous American might. While less effusive, liberal perspectives credit the United States with making noble efforts to advance the cause of a supposedly ordered liberal capitalist world. The patriotic historian is an apologist; the liberal traffics in American exceptionalism lite.

This book, conversely, considers the American history of imperial violence and warfare fundamentally and normatively wrong. Imperialism and militarism dehumanize, repress, and kill people, even as they distort and detract from the pursuit of more enlightened national and global priorities and policies. Imperialism and war should be condemned, transcended, and replaced with a paradigm of cooperative internationalism, a concept that I outline in the Conclusion.

A Note on Sources

This book, my eleventh on American history, is more of a sweeping historical essay than a monograph. It draws on some forty years of reading, teaching, and thinking about the history of the United States and world affairs. All my previous works--as well as this one--have been peer reviewed by established scholars. In the absence of footnotes, readers will have to take my word for it that the factual references and the relatively few quotations interspersed within the text are both genuine and accurate.

Acknowledgements

I would like to thank the Wallace Action Fund and especially Randall Wallace for a generous research grant in support of this project. In addition to my family, I would also like to thank research scholar Grant F. Smith and historian Scott Laderman for their indispensable critical analysis, editorial assistance, and friendship.

.

Chapter 1
Forged by Imperialism and War

The American penchant for imperialism and war began germinating well before the creation of the United States. Beginning a history of the United States or US foreign policy with the Revolution in 1776, as so often occurs, ignores centuries of violent conflict with indigenous people as well as a series of imperial wars. These conflicts powerfully influenced the construction of American national identity and laid the foundation for the US imperial and military history that followed.

In recent times, and long overdue, the year 1619 has been highlighted to mark what some argue should be the real starting point for understanding "American" history. In that year a group of English privateers sold some 20 slaves in the Virginia colony, inaugurating the slave trade in the future United States.

The problem with 1619 as the primary temporal landmark of American history is that even that early date does not go back far enough. The landing of the first African slaves in 1619 did not mark the beginning of racial violence on American shores or even the beginning of slavery, which was ubiquitous in the early modern world. Many Americans are unaware that *Indian* slavery preceded African slavery in North America; or that it was a continent-wide phenomenon accompanied by horrendous and prolonged warfare. American military and imperial history thus began before African slavery with the subjugation and enslavement of indigenous people.

The people who named the US capital city and the capital of the state of Ohio were not wrong: American history begins with Columbus. On his first voyage attempting to reach Asia by sea, Columbus "discovered" what would be called the Americas in honor of a subsequent voyager, Amerigo Vespucci. In 1493 Columbus reported back to the Spanish monarchs—who were also architects of the Spanish Inquisition—that the indigenous people he had encountered were heathens who might however be made into Christians. The guileless natives would also make "good servants."

Columbus claimed the land and the people for the foreign kingdom of Spain and in so doing he established European imperialism on American shores. Wrongly assuming he had arrived in the East Indies, Columbus designated the natives *los Indios*, giving rise to the homogenizing trope of "Indians," which has endured for more than half a millennium. By describing characteristics of the natives, establishing their identity as a separate and inferior group of humanity, Columbus ensconced racial and ethnic difference—civilization vs. savagery--on American shores.

After Columbus came the *conquistadores*, Hernan Cortez and Francisco Pizarro in the lead. In Central and South America, these architects of the Spanish "conquest" (which was a more complex and incomplete project than the term implies) showed that colonization and forced labor paid off, notably in gold and silver.

The next generation of would-be conquistadores enjoyed less success, however. Embarking in 1539 from Cuba, Hernando De Soto went up the West Coast of *la Florida* (named for its flowering beauty). Accompanied by 600 soldiers, he then tramped across the southeast (Georgia, South Carolina, Alabama, Mississippi, Louisiana, Arkansas, and Texas of today) scouring the land for precious metals and other valuable commodities.

De Soto seized some pearls from natives but found little else of value. He regularly unleashed his soldiers and war dogs on the indigenous people, carrying out a series of murderous assaults. "The kind of all-consuming violence that Soto imported was unknown to the chieftains that inhabited the region," historian Matthew Jennings has pointed out. The natives fought back, including a major battle at the future Mobile, Alabama. On May 21, 1542, De Soto died of fever and his body was consigned to the muddy waters of the Mississippi River.

In the wake of De Soto's depredations, and well before African slavery in the future United States, the entire southeast became roiled by wars of Indian slavery. The Indian slave wars raged *for nearly two centuries*, killing thousands of indigenous people who by that time were already dying by the droves from a variety of European diseases for which they lacked immunities and were thus wholly susceptible.

The wars of Indian slavery destroyed Mississippian Indian culture, which had thrived for centuries. Seemingly anchored by the great metropolis at Cahokia, near East St. Louis, Illinois, indigenous culture had radiated in all directions. Mound builders, traders, chieftains and sorcerers connected indigenous bands from modern day Seattle to Florida.

The Europeans did not introduce warfare to indigenous cultures, most of which were led by powerful chieftains who had proven themselves in conflict with other tribes. Warfare, even a "cult of war," was intrinsic to indigenous societies, which fought over hunting grounds and to establish manhood, power and prestige. Indians took prisoners, engaged in ritualistic tortures, and fought wars for blood revenge. Indigenous warfare could be cruel but was typically limited in scope rather than exterminatory.

The point is not that Europeans introduced either slavery or violence to North America, rather that they dramatically expanded these practices, and in the process took a wrecking ball to indigenous culture and indigenous polities. The wars of Indian slavery spurred by the Europeans also left a permanent stamp on "American" identity by entrenching war and imperialism.

Europeans—including now the French, English, and other settlers as well as the Spanish—unleashed a "frenzy of slaving" in which Indian men were seized for forced labor and Indian women (as well as some men and no doubt children) were taken for sexual exploitation. Indigenous bands participated in slave wars, attacking, capturing and trading other Indians for guns, ammunition, liquor, and other European goods. Some Indians were willing participants but over time the bands had little choice: they could either help the European interlopers to enslave other tribes--or become slaves themselves.

As would so often happen throughout the history of American settlement, allying with the Europeans failed to bring indigenous people long-term security. The Tuscarora, for example, allied with Carolina settlers in the slave wars against other tribes, only to have the colonists turn on them in the Tuscarora War (1711-15). Tuscarora refugees fled north and became the sixth band of the Iroquois Confederation, which allied with the British and remained powerful until the Revolutionary War.

Indians dished out punishment of their own in the Yamassee War (1715-17), killing some 400 colonists and slave traders. The Carolina settlers lashed back with genocidal warfare, replete with massacres and scalp bounties, and "destroyed the Yamassees as a political entity." A little more than a decade later the French enslaved the Natchez, the largest tribe in the Mississippi Valley, virtually destroying them as a people.

The imperial slave wars enveloped most of the continent before ebbing in the eighteenth century. Africans, methodically imported in chains from the West Indies following the horrific Middle Passage from the African West Coast, made heartier slaves. Long in contact with Europeans, Africans had acquired immunities to disease. In addition, they could not so easily blend into the countryside when they became runaway slaves.

The massive destruction of the Indian slave wars, especially in what anthropologists have called the Mississippi "shatter zone," are almost beyond comprehension. The prolonged conflict destroyed entire tribes such as the Apalachee, which previously had functioned as a united band for 600 years. In Florida, where hundreds of thousands of Indians had once lived, only a relative-few-refugees survived by escaping to the swamplands.

Through the process of ethnogenesis, however, southeastern Indians reconfigured their identities. Remnants and refugees banded together to form new collectives, including those that would come to be known as the "five civilized tribes"—the Cherokee, Choctaw, Chickasaw, Creek, and Seminole bands. They would thrive for a century—until the Americans

11

under a military hero president orchestrated a new wave of imperial ethnic cleansing.

Genocidal Warfare in the Founding of British America

While most American schoolchildren learn their history as a linear progression from the Atlantic seaboard colonies inward, this framework belies the French and Spanish traders, trappers, friars, soldiers, and adventurers from the Great Lakes to the Southwest. The first "American" settlement was not Jamestown, Virginia, but rather the Spanish fortress at St. Augustine, Florida (1565).

Jamestown has long been the focal point, however, because it was English and because Virginia became so integral—eventually supplying four two-term American presidents of the first five men to hold the office. The initial settlement on the James River was a death trap. The early colonists settled in a malaria swamp, did not know how to gather or grow food, and died in large numbers. Although they viewed the Indians as "heathens" and "salvages," they nonetheless depended on them for survival. Powhatan, the preeminent Indian chieftain, displayed his power in the legendary incident in which he arranged for one of his daughters, Pocahontas, to "save" the English mercenary John Smith from execution in December 1607. Powhatan no doubt later wished he had eliminated Smith when he had the chance.

A veteran of wars in the Balkans against the Islamic Moors, Smith provided the hardened military discipline and ultimately the imperial aggression that anchored the Virginia Company settlement. He viewed the savages as "treacherous" and "infernal hell hounds" but also "quick of apprehension," and "very ingenious." In 1609, when the first all-out war erupted, Smith led a campaign of irregular warfare--which quickly became institutionalized in Virginia--as he burned and razed Indian homes and agricultural fields.

By 1620 the once fledgling colony had grown to 1,000 people and had established a viable economic foundation through cultivation of a profitable cash crop, tobacco. King James criticized the tobacco monoculture, and also urged Christianization of Indians rather than killing them, but this was wishful thinking from a faraway throne.

In 1622 tensions escalated as Opechancanough, Powhatan's successor, realized that the ships would keep coming and the European imperialism would continue to expand onto Indian lands and to destroy their way of life. He launched an all-out assault, killing 347 settlers. The Virginians responded in kind. With genocide on his mind, the governor declared that it would be "infinitely better to have no heathen among us." Smith concurred, "We have just cause to destroy them by all means possible."

The Virginians killed every Indian they could regardless of age or gender before declaring a truce. They surreptitiously served poisoned wine at the subsequent peace talks, leaving some 250 Indians writhing in agony before they were methodically butchered. In 1644 Opechancanough, 90 years old at the time, launched a surprise offensive slaughtering or capturing some 500 settlers, but by this time the local tribes were outnumbered, and Smith and his followers had organized an effective militia. Their search and destroy operations cleansed the tribes from their homelands and brought an end to the brutal Tidewater wars.

As Virginia expanded and settlers continued the imperial takeover of Indian lands, violent conflict was inevitable. Warfare was not the sum total of Euro-American relations with Indians. Colonists traded, allied, Christianized, even married Indians, following the example set by Pocahontas and John Rolfe in 1614. Long periods of peace and relative calm could prevail but ultimately the sheer numbers of settlers produced a demographic swamping that spelled doom for indigenous societies.

Virginia and British authorities were powerless to restrain settler colonialism—essentially the forcible occupation and takeover of indigenous lands--as the pivotal incident known as Bacon's Rebellion (1675-76) illustrated. Unable to inherit land in England, which under primogeniture would go to his older brother, Bacon sailed to Virginia, where he found the best available land had already been taken. Livid when the governor drew a line on settler expansion in an effort to avoid Indian conflict, Bacon decried appeasing the "darling Indians" who were nothing but "barbarous outlaws" and "delinquents" whose interests should never be accommodated over the interests of "his Majesty's loyal subjects."

Defying the governor and the Crown, the charismatic Bacon assembled an irregular army dominated by the white underclass and assaulted Pamunkey and Occaneechi villages in a search and destroy operation. The longtime Virginia Governor William Berkeley tried to rein in Bacon's army but the rebels defeated the militia, burned Jamestown to the ground, and drove Berkeley onto a ship in Jamestown harbor.

Bacon died suddenly, probably from dysentery, and the rebellion eventually collapsed, but the uprising offers many crucial history lessons. First, when push came to shove between settlers and Indians, imperialism would invariably prevail over respect for indigenous land holdings; second, the British-American settlers were beginning to develop a profound disrespect for distant governmental authority, as they preferred to take matters into their own hands on the "frontier"; and third, it was safer to import Afro-Caribbean slaves than to maintain the system of indentured servitude in which white "bound men" had worked for elite planters who dominated the early colonial settlement. Ultimately, Bacon's rebellion showed that poorly educated and economically deprived white men with guns could be very dangerous people in America.

The Genocidal Wars of New England

Virginia and New England could not have been more socially and economically divergent, yet war and imperialism prevailed in both. Planter-led agriculturalists dominated Virginia, whereas New England towns forged by Protestant dissenters and separatists led the other. But both colonies developed a growing frustration with Crown authority—and both ultimately chose to cleanse Indians from the land, including by means of genocidal warfare.

Landing at Cape Cod in 1620, the Pilgrims anticipated troublesome relations with natives but instead received crucial assistance in logistics, fishing, and corn planting. Relations quickly deteriorated, however, amid mutual suspicions. The Plymouth Governor William Bradford concluded that the indigenes were "savage people . . . cruel, barbarous, and most treacherous."

To the north the Puritans of Massachusetts Bay conducted trade and intercultural exchange with Indians in the first years of settlement before turning on the Pequot tribe in a war of annihilation. The anxiety-ridden settlers launched a "holy war" after deciding that the Pequot were hatching "a satanic plot to destroy Christ's church in the wilderness."

In May 1637 the Bay Colony, joined by the Mohegan and the Narragansett, longtime rivals of the Pequot, carried out an exterminatory assault along the Mystic River, killing men, women and children, and burning the Pequot village to the ground. "Sometimes," Captain John Underhill explained in his account of the assault, "the scripture declareth that women and children must perish with their parents . . . We had sufficient light from the Word of God for our proceedings."

The Dutch carried out similar indiscriminate attacks following the infamous purchase of Manhattan for a pittance from the indigenous residents in 1626. Establishing fur trading posts in Albany and New Amsterdam, the Dutch had little choice but to find accommodation with the powerful Iroquois Confederation, which anchored the lucrative beaver trade, but other tribes were more vulnerable. Dismissing the bands whose lands they coveted as "entirely savage and wild," the Dutch summoned the mercenary Underhill to reprise the total war policies he carried out against the Pequot. In 1644 he led an exterminatory expedition of burning villages and slaughtering more than 500 Indians.

14

Not all settlers relished killing Indians; some sought to save their souls. From 1651-74 the Rev. John Eliot established "praying towns" inhabited by more than 1,000 Massachusetts Indians. The settlers also conducted trade and diplomacy with various tribes, but invariably tensions would flare and colonists would decide to rid themselves of the savage people.

Prior to the totalizing violence of King Philip's War (1675-76), the Wampanoag maintained relative equilibrium with the growing Bay Colony under the leadership of Massasoit. After Massasoit's death in 1661 his son and successor Metacomet walked the streets of Boston, trading and interacting with the Puritans, who acknowledged his status by according him the European name King Philip. Although hundreds of Wampanoag had converted to Christianity and engaged in commerce with the settlers, relations deteriorated over encroachments onto Indian fields and hunting grounds as well as violence against the natives. Metacomet grasped that the "insolent" Bay Colony settlers were attempting to "drive us from the graves of our fathers . . . and enslave our women and children."

Metacomet launched his own war of annihilation, methodically marching from town to town and leaving them littered with dead and mutilated bodies amid smoldering ruins. Families were massacred and churches torched. More than 500 militiamen and some 1,000 civilians died in King Philip's War--the highest death toll in the entire history of "American" warfare, in proportion to population.

New England communities mobilized—men, women, and children— in the campaign against the "savages." Graphic narratives recounted Indian captivity, torture, scalping, and mutilation of settler victims. In a famous account the settler Mary Rowlandson described an attack on her home in 1675 by the "bloody heathen" who killed men, women, and children, including shooting to death the baby she held in her arms before taking her captive. Her account circulated throughout the colonies reinforcing notions of helpless women and maidens confronting violent assaults on their families including the specter of sexual assault, the proverbial "fate worse than death" at the hands of the savages. These captivity narratives obscured that to the indigenous bands of North America taking prisoners was a normal accompaniment to warfare. Indians took captives to adopt and replace those who had died of disease or warfare, thus to "cover the dead." Indians also exchanged captives through diplomacy to facilitate bringing an end to conflict.

The settlers ultimately prevailed in King Philip's War but not before hundreds of people had died and many towns were destroyed. Many New Englanders now viewed all Indians as a "brutish enemy" that should be driven from the land if not exterminated. Colonists from Massachusetts, Rhode Island, and Connecticut created a new Army of the United Colonies. The military force embarked on search and destroy missions, including attacks on the praying towns the Puritans had established. In December 1675 the "Great Swamp Fight" near Kingston, Rhode Island, was in reality a massacre of some 500 Narragansett, mostly women and children.

In August 1676 the settler army tracked down and killed Metacomet. They ordered the body of the "great naked, dirty beast" drawn and quartered, severed his head and placed it on display atop a pole outside Plymouth, where the skull remained perched for decades. More than 3,000 Indians died, including some executed after the war, and others, including "Philip's" nine-year-old son, were sold into slavery. The New England Indian communities never recovered from the war. They declined in population while the colonists rebuilt and continued to unload ship after ship of new settlers and supplies.

Imperialism and warfare continued across the eighteenth century between Euro-American settlers and indigenous people attempting to defend their homelands and way of life. But colonists did not fight solely with Indians—the Europeans also carried on a long-term, high stakes imperial rivalry in which control of the North American continent was the ultimate prize.

The Imperial Wars

From the late seventeenth century to 1763 a series of imperial wars rocked the British-American colonies. Britain, France and Spain were the primary players in conflicts fueled by the zero-sum mentality of mercantile competition for control of world trade exacerbated by Protestant-Catholic enmities. The nations battled on land and sea, over fisheries, the fur trade, lucrative sugar islands built on slave labor, and much else.

Indigenous bands entered into military alliances with Europeans in return for tools, muskets, powder and liquor, but they rarely achieved security for their own homelands. Many indigenous people absorbed European ideas, and some converted to Christianity.

From their base in Quebec the French encouraged assaults by the Abenaki and other tribes onto the English settlements in Maine. Embracing *la petite guerre* (guerrilla war), the French and their Indian allies terrorized New England villages amid King William's War. They killed hundreds of people in New York, New Hampshire, Maine, and Massachusetts.

Ended by treaty in 1697, King William's War proved inconclusive, but the English colonists had learned they could not depend on the Crown to protect their homes. As the war unfolded the monarchy had shown more concern about the fighting in Europe and thus refused requests to send sufficient numbers of troops to protect the colonists from French and Indian attacks. Accordingly, the imperative to mobilize a well-armed populace gained ground on American shores.

War and imperial rivalry carried into the new century in Queen Anne's War (1702-13) and King George's War (1740-48). The decisive phase of imperial conflict, known as the Seven Years War in Europe and the French and Indian War in North America, was more violent than the previous wars. In many respects this was also the first truly global war. Yet the crucial theater--where the war began and where the stakes were highest-- was in North America.

In 1754 a clash in the Pennsylvania backcountry set off the world war. Exploiting their strategic presence in the interior of the continent, the French sought to cut off English westward expansion. English settlers and land speculators had set their sights on the Ohio Valley, but the French built a series of outposts culminating in Fort Duquesne located at the "forks" of the Ohio River (modern day Pittsburgh) to block the British colonials. The French drove out the Virginia militia, forcing the surrender of a young regimental leader, George Washington.

Advised to consult with the local tribes about strategy and tactics for navigating the Pennsylvania woodlands, British General Edward Braddock met with the Delaware leader Shingas, who dangled a potential alliance in return for security guarantees for the Delaware homelands. Braddock responded contemptuously, telling the Indian leader, "No savage shall inherit the land." The imperious British martinet told Benjamin Franklin that while Indians in league with the French might pose a threat to the "raw American militia," they would quickly succumb in any encounter with "the King's regular and disciplined troops."

Braddock soon learned how wrong he was, but it was his last lesson in life. Cutting a path through the woods, Braddock and his forces crossed the Monongahela River above Fort Duquesne whereupon a combined force of French and Indians poured out of the woods and slaughtered them. Braddock was among the first mortally wounded in the massacre in which the British took 914 casualties against 23 French dead and only dozens wounded. Washington again narrowly escaped with his life.

The British suffered a series of ensuing defeats, including the loss of Fort William Henry on Lake George in 1757. Surrounded by French and Indian forces, the British accepted terms and began to march out in surrender. The French commander Marquis de Montcalm could not control his indigenous allies, however, as they had not agreed to the European-style honorable surrender. The indigenous culture of warfare demanded making contact with the enemy, killing and taking captives and trophies from the field. The braves had not paddled and tramped scores of miles to preside over some orderly European surrender ceremony. The

Abenaki, Ottawa, Potawatomi, among others, thus descended on the defenseless people who had filed out of the fort, killing 185 and taking 300-500 captives, men, women and children.

By this time the borderlands were aflame with conflict, as Indians lashed back at vulnerable settlers who had continued to move inexorably onto indigenous lands and hunting grounds. The elite Penn family, devout Quakers, originally envisioned their woodlands as a vast arena of peaceful cooperation between settlers and Indians—all of whom after all possessed the "inner light" of God, or so the Friends believed. While professing to respect the Indians' humanity, Penn nonetheless authorized land sales that eroded their way of life. The new phase of imperial warfare, the arrogance shown by Braddock and others, now ignited a wave of terrifying violence. Indians descended on homes and farms and killed indiscriminately across the borderlands. Narratives of "barbarian" and "savage" slaughter and captivity pervaded a graphic colonial discourse that included vivid descriptions of "bashed-in skulls and cut-out tongues . . . of sharp objects stuck in eyes and genitals."

The turning point in the imperial war came in 1757 when William Pitt took power and deviated from the traditional Europe-first strategy. Pitt poured money and troops into North America and advised the British to show some respect for colonial militias and Indian allies. As the British dug out a new road into the backcountry, the French departed Fort Duquesne and burned it to the ground, leaving the British to resurrect "Fort Pitt."

In 1758 the British had brought a measure of calm to the borderlands by making concessions to the Indians at the Treaty of Easton, but the peace did not hold. As the settler population continued to grow—it had more than quadrupled to 1.2 million from 1700-1750—indigenous homelands and hunting grounds were overrun. Violence between settlers and the indigenous bands was sporadic but endemic.

In 1759 Major-General Robert Rogers of Massachusetts—accredited today as the founder of the American Army Ranger tradition—recruited a force of mostly Scotch-Irish irregulars to assault the hated Abenaki in their villages north of Montreal. Invited by his commanders to show "no mercy," Rogers complied in spades, attacking the vulnerable village at dawn and perpetrating a massacre. Noting myriad Euro-American scalps wafting in the village breeze, the attackers unleashed a pitiless assault. Most of the Abenaki warriors were gone, however, leaving scores if not hundreds of old men, women and children to burn to death in their homes or be slaughtered as they escaped them.

Indigenous bands, particularly those that had allied with the French, realized that the sweeping British victory left them imperiled, as they were no longer able to play off one European power against the other.

Furthermore, while the French had lived in the interior with Indians, a situation in which many Frenchmen married into the tribes and thus came to understand Indian culture and diplomacy, especially the importance of mutual respect and gift-giving, the British displayed ignorance and contempt. British generals had no enthusiasm for gift-giving and instead built a series of forts in the northwest to pave the way for increased Anglo expansion into Indian country.

In the southeast tribes such as the Cherokee and the Catawba who had helped defeat the French found the British ungrateful and the settlers no less determined to squat on their homelands. British Commander Jeffrey Amherst, contemptuous of the savages, ordered indiscriminate assaults during the so-called Cherokee War of 1758-61. British-Americans laid waste the Cherokee villages, sparing no one, and summarily executed 22 chiefs who met with them to seek a negotiated settlement. The Catawba were violently removed from their Carolina upcountry homelands and relegated to a small reserve.

Warned that indigenous frustrations were on the verge of boiling over into a continent-wide uprising, Amherst declared that the tribes lacked the "capacity of attempting anything serious." If they tried to mount a resistance, he vowed to "punish the delinquents with entire destruction." Like Braddock and many others, Amherst had badly underestimated the natives.

In the spring of 1763, a broad coalition of indigenous bands launched attacks on forts and settlements throughout the borderlands. They reciprocated the indiscriminate killing of Redcoats as well as settlers. Dubbed "Pontiac's Rebellion," for an Ottawa chieftain, the conflict was a pan-Indian campaign of homeland cultural defense.

Apoplectic after being proven wrong, Amherst responded by advocating genocide. It was time, he declared, to "extirpate this execrable race . . . I wish to hear of no prisoners." He followed up by authorizing biological warfare by means of sending blankets and cloth infected with smallpox into Indian communities.

Violent Indian resistance traumatized settlers, inflamed public opinion, and led to campaigns of dispossession backed by indiscriminate violence. The colonial press routinely referenced Indian resistance as "murder" and "massacre" perpetrated by "barbarians" and "savages." Violence raged across the borderlands, as the settlers, as one English trader put it, "thought it a meritorious act to kill Heathens wherever they are found." The Pennsylvania governor declared the colony a free fire zone, authorizing the "taking, killing, or destroying" of Indians. The practice of offering bounties to scalp hunters whose targets included Indian women and children proliferated. In December 1763 near Lancaster, a mob known as the Paxton boys seized 14 Susquehannock Indians from protective custody to slaughter and mutilate them.

As the American colonial rebellion unfolded in the 1760s, settlers continued to stream into the western and southern borderlands in defiance of British authority. Many of these settlers had lost family and friends to Indian raids and otherwise displayed racial contempt for people they considered heathen savages who were un-fit to hold the land. More and more the settlers identified themselves as "white" people destined to inhabit the spaces claimed by an inferior race.

The momentum of violent Indian removal and resistance to British authority came from the bottom up and from the top down—from common people as well as colonial elites. More than 50,000 settlers lived on the trans-Appalachian borderlands, beyond the reach of colonial authorities. British officials described these settlers and squatters as "low" and "the very dregs of the people." They declared that they were "too numerous, too lawless and licentious ever to be restrained." Land speculators joined the settlers in advocating the removal of Indians and defiance of British decrees limiting expansion. Future leaders of the American Revolution—Washington, Patrick Henry, and Thomas Jefferson among them—were deeply involved in land speculation.

In an effort to rein in settlers and squatters, the Crown issued the Royal Proclamation (1763) forbidding new land grants on the Western side of the Appalachian range, reiterating a pledge made to the tribes at the Treaty of Easton. Having just ended a total war with the French, and wracked by indebtedness, the British were trying to bring a halt to the brutal borderland conflict.

British diplomacy soothed Indian rage but ignited the fury of the colonists. The effort to restrict mobility and settlement, followed up by a series of new tax levies--under which the colonists, not unreasonably, were asked to help generate the revenue needed to address the war debt and fund their own defense--set off a general rebellion rooted in New England. Ironically, the sweeping British victory in the decisive phase of the imperial wars was leading directly to the American Revolution.

The Revolutionary War

War nearly always brings unintended consequences, a truism clearly borne out in the aftermath of the French and Indian War. Allowed substantial leeway for decades to govern their own affairs during an era of "salutary neglect," the colonies were suddenly directed to draw a line on settlement and raise revenue through internal taxation. Rebellion erupted immediately, began to spin out of control with the feverish reaction to the Stamp Act (1765), and reached a point of no return a decade later.

New England and especially Boston emerged as the center of the revolt. The "Boston massacre" (1770), in which British troops fired into a crowd killing five protesters, galvanized the opposition to Crown rule. The famous "tea party" protests followed in 1773. As the colonial militia cached arms and mobilized for resistance, the British Army went on the offensive at Lexington and Concord. In June 1775 full-scale warfare erupted outside Boston at Breed's and Bunker Hills. At the end of 1775 the Americans invaded Canada, on the assumption that the northern colonies would join them in rebellion, but the assault on Quebec ended in total defeat.

Under the command of the Virginian Washington, who lacked formal military training but had gained considerable experience in the French and Indian conflict, the Continental Army surrounded the British at the center of the maelstrom in Boston. In March 1776 Washington reluctantly agreed to allow the British to vacate the city, which they otherwise had vowed to burn to the ground.

Meeting at their capital in Philadelphia in July, the Americans declared their independence behind the radical notion that "all men are created equal." The declaration listed the grievances on the part of the Crown that had sought to usurp their "unalienable rights." Thomas Paine raised popular support for the rebellion with his brilliant propaganda tract "Common Sense," yet a majority of people in the 13 colonies remained either loyal to the Crown or undecided.

Embittered by the violent unrest, but certain they would quell it through application of the overwhelming might of the empire, the British put into effect a strategy in which they would seize New York and shore up the widespread loyal support in the southern colonies. All the talk of men being created equal posed a rhetorical threat to slavery, the lifeblood of the planation economies. The British planned to silence such talk by blockading the American coasts, surrounding and eventually crushing the rebellion in New England, and by rounding up and hanging the traitorous rebel leaders.

Washington realized that the Americans would have to fight a guerrilla war of harassment and hit and run resistance, carefully picking the spots for more traditional battles lest his fledgling army be overwhelmed by the superior British forces. The British were less skilled at counter-insurgency warfare and would require vast superiority in numbers to defeat the rebellion. For this reason, they imported Hessian mercenaries to help subdue the rebels.

With public support in the balance in the wake of defeats in Canada and New York, Washington desperately sought to reclaim momentum for the rebellion. With that purpose in mind, he pulled off the surprise attack on Trenton following a rugged wintry march and risky crossing of the Delaware River on Christmas night 1776. The following day Washington's troops caught a large Hessian mercenary force by surprise and killed and imprisoned hundreds of them in a total rout. Days later the Continental Army prevailed in a follow-up battle at Princeton.

The victories were just what the Americans needed to preserve morale and revivify the revolutionary spirit, but what they ultimately required in order to win the war was foreign assistance and alliance, namely from France. Bitter over their defeat in the decisive imperial war, the French nonetheless remained leery of the rebel prospects, even as Franklin and other envoys attempted to win them over through diplomacy in Paris.

The defeats in New Jersey were annoying but the British controlled the seas, enjoyed support in the southern colonies, and were on the move down Lake Champlain, forcing the rebels to abandon Fort Ticonderoga without a fight. At this point the British General John Burgoyne overextended his forces, which were soon surrounded at Saratoga. Cut off from supply lines, and with the New York winter closing in, it became clear that "Gentleman Johnny," who had once penned a comic opera, had now orchestrated a British tragedy, as he had no choice but to surrender his 6,000-man army in the biggest defeat of the war in October 1777.

Victory at Saratoga had an electrifying effect on American public opinion but moreover convinced the French to take the plunge into alliance and belligerency. Spain and Holland later entered on the American side as well. With the promise of great power assistance, the American Revolution had been transformed from a longshot into a genuine possibility.

The British were hardly defeated after Saratoga but would have to concentrate their forces on the southern colonies while maintaining the occupation of New York. The British carried out their southern strategy, seizing the key port cities of Savannah and Charleston, solidifying their control of the Atlantic seaboard. In 1780 the Redcoats won a major victory on the battlefield at Camden, South Carolina.

Increasingly draconian British occupation policies alienated key constituencies and fueled the rise of partisan support for the Revolution in the southern colonies. While the British controlled the port cities, partisans took command of the countryside through hit and run attacks, sabotage, and disruption of supply lines. The classic guerrilla warfare began to wear down the occupation and occasionally produced major victories on the battlefield, as at Cowpens, South Carolina in January 1781, a turning point in the war in the south.

Encamped at Yorktown on the Virginia side of Chesapeake Bay, Lord Charles Cornwallis's army became entrapped in a land-sea pincer.

Surrounded on land by the partisan militias, the Continental Army and a sizeable French force, the British also lost the battle of the Chesapeake at sea. Cornwallis had little choice but to surrender some 8,000 troops, ships, and cannon at Yorktown in October 1781. The British had suffered a defeat from which they could not recover.

At one point early in the war Washington had mused it would take "almost a miracle" to survive the conflict with Great Britain, but through a combination of revolutionary fervor, guerrilla warfare, and with the help of the enemies of Britain—which had no major allies beyond the Iroquois Confederation—the "miracle" had come to pass.

The United States--like the Vietnamese resistance in a future guerrilla war--won by outlasting the enemy. Britain still occupied the two major cities of North America, Philadelphia and New York, and remained dominant at sea—but the British had larger concerns amid another war that had gone global. They focused on ensuring the security of the lucrative sugar producing islands Jamaica and Barbados and other Caribbean possessions as well as Mediterranean and Asian outposts of empire. They could not afford to continue what had clearly become an inconclusive counterinsurgency conflict with the ebullient rebels. As with the Americans later in Vietnam and Afghanistan, the British could not secure the countryside where they continued to lose ground. It was time to bring the war to an end.

The Americans got everything they wanted at the Treaty of Paris (1783), including fishing rights, British assurance that American slaves would not be liberated and removed, and most significantly, national boundaries to the Mississippi River, which set the stage for the coming American campaigns of ethnic cleansing of the indigenous population.

"Merciless Indian Savages"

The Americans were the big winners in the Revolutionary War, but the biggest losers were not the British, who remained a powerful global empire, but rather the indigenous tribes, which now confronted a relentlessly expanding republic. Downplayed in traditional histories of the Revolutionary War, which is typically framed narrowly as a fight for freedom against colonial oppression, Indian removal was a driving force in the conflict from start to finish.

The Royal Proclamation, which outraged settlers as well as elite land speculators, ignited the colonial rebellion in 1763. In listing their grievances against King George whilst proclaiming independence in 1776, the Americans condemned the monarch who had "endeavored to bring on the Inhabitants of our Frontiers, the merciless Indian Savages whose known Rule of Warfare, is an undistinguished Destruction of all Ages, Sexes and Conditions."

Prior to the outbreak of the Revolution, the Virginia governor Lord Dunmore overturned royal decrees against speculation in Indian lands thus enabling surveyors and settlers to pour into Kentucky. The action precipitated Dunmore's War (1774) in which drunken settlers slaughtered Indians for sport. The murders compelled the Mingo chief Logan, long an advocate of coexistence with whites, to kill 13 settlers in a proportionate act of blood revenge, to which Dunmore responded by declaring that any and all Indians should be "severely chastised." It was open season on Kentucky Indians and their lands.

In 1777 Cornstalk, a distinguished Shawnee chief, traveled to Point Pleasant on the far western Virginia borderlands in an effort to rein in the violence. A settler mob responded to the peace mission by executing and mutilating Cornstalk and his son. Kentucky and Ohio Indians thereafter fought the Americans to the death, defeating them in August 1782 at Blue Licks in the last substantial battle of the Revolutionary War.

Well aware of the threat posed by the Americans, the Iroquois Confederation, the most powerful indigenous group, allied with the British in an effort to maintain their homelands in the Finger Lakes region of New York. In July 1778 in the Wyoming Valley of northeastern Pennsylvania, a combined British and Iroquois force descended on the rebel stronghold of Wilkes-Barre, slaughtering 227 settlers while taking only five prisoners. The next year, with the war turning in their favor, the Americans took their revenge on the Iroquois. Acting on Washington's orders, General John Sullivan razed some 40 villages in the Iroquois heartland of upstate New York. The expedition, Sullivan reported to Washington, brought "total ruin of the Indian settlement, and the destruction of their crops, which were designed for the support of those inhuman barbarians, while they were desolating the American frontiers."

Blaming the British for inciting the "merciless savages" on the borderlands, the Americans fought against both enemies. In February 1779 Colonel George Rogers Clark, who believed the only way to deal with the tribes was "to excel them in barbarity," carried out a macabre execution in an effort to make an impression on the British territorial governor Henry Hamilton, dubbed the "hair-buyer" for his support of Indian attacks.

After surrounding the British at their fort in Vincennes in the Indiana Territory, Clark bludgeoned an Ottawa Indian prisoner, Macutté Mong, in the sight of the British, letting them know what would happen if they failed to surrender. After being struck in the head with a tomahawk, Mong handed the weapon back to Clark, mocking his failure to kill him, which Clark then proceeded to do. With his "hands and face still reeking of the human sacrifice," as Hamilton put it, Clark took the surrender of the fort and told Hamilton that as to Indians "for his part he would never spare man, woman or child of them."

A growing number of American settlers could perceive Indians only as "merciless savages" in need of extermination. "On this side of the mountain," one American acknowledged, "the country talks of nothing but killing Indians and taking possession of their lands."

In March 1782 settlers perpetrated a genocidal massacre, perhaps the most egregious in all American history, at Gnadenhutten, a Moravian Christian mission for Delaware Indians near the Pennsylvania border within the Ohio country. Militiamen from Virginia and Pennsylvania found the pacifist Indian converts harvesting a corn crop left behind in the fall. The militiamen took a vote in which they decided to summarily execute all 96 Indians, including 39 children. After an evening of wailing, song, and prayer, they were forced to kneel, one after another, and were bludgeoned to death. One teenager survived amid the carnage.

Asked by a Moravian missionary why they had slaughtered the non-combative Indian converts, who had posed no threat, one of the militiamen explained, "When they killed the Indians the country would be theirs, and the sooner this was done the better."

Chapter 2
"Destined" for Imperialism and War

Victory in the Revolutionary War enabled American imperialism to flourish on the North American borderlands. Under the drives inherent in settler colonization, Americans would take land from indigenous people, peacefully if possible, by violence if deemed necessary.

In the Treaty of Paris (1783), Britain recognized a vast swath of US territory extending to the Mississippi River. The indigenous residents of the land were not consulted in the white man's diplomacy, did not consent to the loss of their homelands and would fight to retain them.

Americans justified Indian removal as the march of progress on the part of a superior white, civilized and Christian nation destined to lead the world into a new age of republicanism. "The Indian will ever retreat as our settlements advance upon them," Washington explained in 1783. "The gradual extension of our settlements will gradually cause the savage as the wolf to retire; both being beasts of prey though they differ in shape."

As a surveyor and speculator in western lands, Washington like other "founding fathers" thus dehumanized Indians and sought to drive them from the land in order to secure US borders. By occupying and converting Indian land into private property, Americans could generate the revenue needed to retire the Revolutionary War debt, at the same time winning the support for the new government from white settlers and land speculators.

Under the new Constitution in 1787 the Congress assumed the prerogative to "regulate commerce with foreign nations . . . and with the Indian tribes." Indians in reality were themselves "foreign nations," but Euro-Americans would not acknowledge the legitimacy or even the humanity of "merciless savages." Asserting that the tribes forfeited land rights because some of them had sided with the British in the Revolutionary War, the United States "negotiated" a series of coerced treaties, which provided a veneer of legality to the dispossession. The United States informed the Iroquois, who had long dominated the Finger Lakes region of New York, that they were a "subdued people" and that the Americans would "dispose of the lands as we think proper or more convenient to ourselves," as General Philip Schuyler bluntly put it.

In the Northwest Ordinance (1787), under which the United States plotted orderly settlement of vast tracts of land (the future states of Ohio,

Indiana, Illinois, Michigan, and Wisconsin), Congress declared that "the utmost good faith shall always be observed towards the Indians." Their "lands and property shall not be taken from them without their consent" and "they shall never be invaded or disturbed, unless in justified and lawful wars authorized by the Congress."

While the reference to "lawful wars" was an important caveat, many of the founders hoped to avoid conflict with Indians by means of treaties and controlled settlement. Yet most accords with Indians, like the Treaty of Fort McIntosh (1785), which opened up vast tracts of Indian-occupied land in Ohio for settlement, were achieved by means of fraud and extortion rather than by mutual understanding.

The dispossession of indigenous people proceeded from the bottom up as well as the top down. As in Bacon's Rebellion more than a century earlier, settlers and squatters felt empowered to take land from Indians with or without government consent. The "frontier miscreants" could be "far more savage and revengeful than the Indians," noted Timothy Pickering, Indian commissioner of the United States in 1790. Many Americans considered "the killing of Indians in time of peace to be no crime," he added.

As settlers laid claim to the "frontier," irregular warfare raged throughout the 1780s and early 1790s. Across the Upper South, the Cherokee, led by Dragging Canoe, put up a fierce resistance to the Americans. Settlers waged a guerrilla war with the Cherokee, who were often in alliance with other tribes such as the Creek (Muskogee), from the Revolutionary War to the mid-1790s.

From Kentucky, American settlers and military commanders invaded the Indian country north of the Ohio River and as far west as the Illinois territory. In 1786 Generals Benjamin Logan and George Rogers Clark led raids in which they razed the villages of the Shawnee and other tribes, killing noncombatants in the process. As Indians fought back, the Northwest Indian Wars or alternatively the Ohio Indian Wars, erupted.

In 1790, near the modern-day Ohio-Indiana border, a coalition led by the Miami under Little Turtle and the Shawnee under Blue Jacket repulsed a European-style traditional assault led by Army General Josiah Harmar. Angered by the defeat, the Americans avowed "vengeance" and the "utter destruction" of the Indian coalition but instead endured the worst defeat suffered by the United States Army in the entire history of Indian warfare. Like General George Armstrong Custer less than a century hence, the Americans badly underestimated the ability of the tribes to amass a fighting force sufficient to win victory on the battlefield.

On November 4, 1791, US forces under General Arthur St. Clair were completely routed in the Battle of the Wabash. The army suffered 650 killed—two and a half times the number that would be killed in Custer's last stand--including 69 of 124 commissioned officers. The Indians stuffed the mouths of the dead with dirt, showing their contempt for the settlers' lust for their land. Some 270 Americans were wounded, including women and children who traveled with the army. The tribes had suffered only 21 dead warriors and 40 wounded in their resounding victory.

Little Turtle, the astute leader of the Miami Confederation, realized, however, that the Indians eventually would be overwhelmed by the sheer number of settlers. The "pale faces" were "like the leaves of the trees. When the frost comes, they fall and are blown away. But when the sunshine comes again, they come back more plentiful than ever before."

Sobered by the humiliating defeat on the Wabash, the Washington administration authorized a massive (at the time) $1 million appropriation, enabling General "Mad" Anthony Wayne to mobilize, train, and equip a force of 2,200 soldiers backed by 1,500 Kentucky volunteers. Wayne methodically constructed a series of forts while drilling his Legion for the march across Ohio.

Waging a campaign of counterinsurgency warfare, Wayne's rangers torched Indian cornfields and villages, scalping and mutilating the residents across the Miami and Maumee River valleys. On August 20, 1794, the campaign culminated in the Battle of Fallen Timbers where the tribes were routed near modern-day Toledo, Ohio. The next year the British agreed in the Jay Treaty to honor the 1783 Paris Treaty commitment to withdraw from their forts on the borderlands, leaving the tribes bereft of allies and unable to resist the Yankee invasion. In the Treaty of Greenville (1795) the Indian coalition signed off on the loss of their homelands, marking the end of the Northwest Indian War. From 1796 to 1810 the settler population of Ohio soared from 5,000 to 230,000.

First Clashes Overseas

As American imperialism uprooted indigenous people on the "frontier," the nation undertook halting efforts to cultivate a national military establishment. Classical republicanism, seemingly confirmed by the experiences of living under British colonialism, condemned standing armies, linking them with taxation and domestic tyranny. A large military, Thomas Paine presciently advised, would promote chauvinism and oppression at home because the state "will have no excuse for its enormous revenue and taxation, except it can prove that, somewhere or other it has enemies."

Military ill-preparedness, leading to the disastrous defeat on the Wabash, as well as American helplessness in the face of superior British and French naval power, however, led to the growing conviction that the

United States needed a more powerful military establishment. In 1794, after intense debate, Congress authorized construction of a six-frigate navy. In 1798 Congress established the Navy Department as separate from the War Department and also established the Marine Corps.

By that time tensions with revolutionary France, which was again at war with Great Britain, took the Americans to the brink of direct overseas conflict. The French, officially still an ally under the 1778 alliance, bitterly resented the US rapprochement with Great Britain under the Jay Treaty. France insulted American diplomatic emissaries (the XYZ Affair of 1797) and ignored American demands for free trade and neutral rights at sea, which included commerce with Britain and its allies.

The undeclared Quasi War with France encompassed clashes among privateers and a few ship-to-ship naval battles. The Convention of 1800 brought an end to the conflict. The agreement formally ended the 1778 alliance while the United States abandoned all claims for damages to shipping. The Quasi War thus concluded with only a few deaths in battle, though hundreds had been wounded in the sea clashes.

Another casualty of the conflict was freedom of speech. For the first but not the last time, the "natural rights" that the Americans had added in the first ten amendments to their historic Constitution came under siege in wartime. The Alien and Sedition Acts (1798) targeted critics of the war, defenders of France and the French alliance, and recent immigrants. Citizens and recent immigrants were variously jailed and deported for questioning national policy. The new laws demonstrated that wartime would foster a hostile climate, undermining civil liberties, a phenomenon that would play out repeatedly over the course of American history.

The election of 1800 brought Jefferson, long suspicious of centralized government and state militarism, to the presidency. However, the sage of Monticello seemed more comfortable with centralized power as long as he and not a British monarch or a Federalist Party leader was wielding it. In 1802 Jefferson authorized the creation of the US Military Academy at West Point, New York. Jefferson also bolstered the Navy, but he concentrated on coastal defense and patrolling of internal waterways. The Virginian authorized a program of constructing smaller gunboats rather than larger warships. The gunboats, 177 of which were built, were smaller and cheaper and construction was spread among the states to bolster political support for Jefferson's Republican Party. It would not be the last time that federal spending on the military within individual states bolstered support for national military policy.

Jefferson sent American frigates and some of the smaller gunboats to the North African "Barbary coast" in response to piratical assaults victimizing US merchant ships and captive seamen. The US ships clashed repeatedly with the North African raiders, but the outcome of the

Tripolitan War (1801-05) was inconclusive, as the United States continued to pay bribes to secure the release of its ships and crewmen. The Navy gained experience in the conflict and the Marine Corps took pride in its actions "on the shores of Tripoli," as later immortalized in its martial hymn.

Closer to home Jefferson adopted a paternal discourse toward Indians, referencing them as "children" who would gradually be assimilated within the United States, yet at the same time he laid the foundation for a century of violent ethnic cleansing of the continent. Under his signal achievement, the Louisiana Purchase (1803) from France, the United States laid claim to more than 530 million acres in the heart of the continent stretching from the Mississippi River to the Rocky Mountains.

Long celebrated as a brilliant real estate deal, the Louisiana Purchase was in reality a landmark in the history of American imperialism. As with the Treaty of Paris in 1783, Europeans and Americans once again asserted illegitimate authority over the inhabited homelands of hundreds of thousands of indigenous people. For the next 90 years American settlers and the Army would violently remove them from their homes and hunting grounds. The Louisiana Purchase thus enabled nearly a century of what would today be considered war crimes and crimes against humanity under international law. The Purchase also affirmed the discourse of American exceptionalism and the nation's "destiny" to lay claim to the entire North American continent.

Another War with Britain

Attacks on American shipping and violations of neutral rights at sea remained the focus of the foreign and military policy of the early republic. The assaults led ultimately to another war with the mother country, Great Britain. Locked in a fight to the death, neither Napoleonic France nor Great Britain were inclined to respect American neutral rights. While France had the dominant land army in Europe, the British sought to exploit their dominant sea power to blockade the French. In order to maintain its domination of the seas the British needed a steady supply of sailors, which encouraged the practice of impressment: forcibly removing sailors from foreign ships. The British targeted American vessels because they regularly recruited experienced British-born sailors.

Impressment was an affront to American neutral rights but moreover to the young nation's pride, as underscored in the humiliating attack on the USS *Chesapeake*. Departing from Hampton Roads, Virginia, for the Mediterranean on June 22, 1807, the 40-gun frigate was promptly intercepted by the 50-gun British warship *Leopard*, which delivered three massive broadsides when the American ship refused to heave to for boarding. After forcing the surrender of the ship, the British removed four seamen from the *Chesapeake*, impressing three and executing one as a deserter.

In 1812 the United States, having exhausted its patience with inconclusive diplomacy, started a full-scale war over the affronts to its neutral rights and national pride. James Madison became the first President to establish the precedent of asking the Congress to fulfill its constitutional prerogative to declare war. Madison could not know that on the eve of war the British had decided to withdraw the orders-in-council that sanctioned impressment tactics targeting the United States, thus obviating the *casus belli*.

In mid-June 1812 Congress declared war by votes of 79-49 in the House and 19-13 in the Senate. Despite the enthusiasm of the War Hawks from the southern and Western states, the United States was internally divided and wholly unprepared for war with the leading power in the world. Congress initially appropriated few funds, leaving the armed forces deficient and dependent on untrained volunteers. None of this stopped the Americans from taking the offensive by again, as in the Revolutionary War, mounting an invasion of Canada, whose residents they wrongly assumed would rise up to throw off British colonialism.

In August 1814 the United States endured a humiliation far worse than anything that might have been imagined when the Chesapeake affair had inflamed the embers of war. The British made landfall, marched into Washington, and looted and burned the executive mansion as well as the Treasury, State, and War departments. At the executive mansion, which had been hastily vacated by the President and Dolley Madison, the British soldiers took time out to enjoy some fresh grilled meat and the finest selections from the presidential wine cellar.

Britain's renewed belligerence in the United States presented indigenous tribes with renewed opportunity to mobilize homeland defense against American imperial aggression. In the Indiana Territory the Shawnee brothers Tenskwatawa (The Prophet) and Tecumseh anchored, respectively, the spiritual and military resistance to a US dispossession campaign led by the territorial Governor William Henry Harrison. In November 1811, with Tecumseh having removed to the south to recruit Indian allies, the Shawnee fought Harrison's forces to a standstill in the Battle of Tippecanoe before they ran out of ammunition and vacated Prophetstown, burning it behind them. The Americans claimed a great victory but the Indian coalition was intact and soon buoyed by the arrival of the British.

With the aid of the Indian allies, the British drove the Americans out of Canada and followed up by surrounding the US fort at Detroit, which ignominiously surrendered in August 1812. The British also took forts at Michilimackinac, at the pivot of the Great Lakes, and Dearborn, near modern day Chicago. In January 1813 the British culminated the onslaught by soundly defeating the Americans in a major battle at River Raisin on the eastern border of the Michigan Territory. To celebrate the victory, Britain's Indian allies drank a case of whiskey and then massacred some 30 to 50 American survivors of the battle.

The Americans had no chance of mounting an effective opposition at sea against the superior British Navy, but as in the Revolutionary War they won just often enough on the ground to stave off a British victory in the war. Led by the 27-year-old Navy Commander Oliver Hazard Perry, the United States won the crucial Battle of Lake Erie in September 1813, reversing the momentum of the war in the northwest. Unwilling to endure heavy losses, the British surrendered Detroit and abandoned their Indian allies. Tecumseh declared bitterly that the British were "like a fat animal that carries its tail upon its back" until frightened, at which time it "drops its tail between its legs and runs off." The American victory in October at the Battle of the Thames, where Tecumseh was killed and left mutilated on the battlefield, devastated the Indian confederacy that had been rekindled by the return of the British only to be abandoned by them once again, as in the Revolutionary War.

To the south the Tennessee militia leader Andrew Jackson capitalized on a civil war raging among the Creeks (Muskogee). The band was divided between the more propertied, mix-blooded and "civilized" Upper Creeks, and the Lower Creeks, also known as the Red Sticks, who embraced Tecumseh's call for indigenous people to mobilize a pan-Indian resistance against the Americans. In March 1814 Jackson's forces, backed by Creek and Choctaw Indian allies, trapped the Red Sticks and slaughtered some 500 of them. Jackson ordered his men to cut off the noses of the dead Indians to assure an accurate count of bodies on the battlefield at the Horseshoe Bend of the Tallapoosa River in modern-day Alabama. In the ensuing Treaty of Fort Jackson, the United States orchestrated a massive dispossession of the Creeks--including the lands of those who had fought *with* Jackson.

Rewarded for his victory, Jackson received a regular Army commission, promotion to major general, and was ordered to take command of US forces in New Orleans. On January 1, 1815, the British launched an ill-conceived frontal assault on the well-fortified US positions in the Crescent City. In a little more than an hour some 300 British soldiers fell dead along with 1,200 wounded and 480 captured in a ringing American victory in the final battle of the war—a war that the combatants had no way of knowing had already ended.

By the time of the slaughter in New Orleans, British and American negotiators in Ghent, Belgium had agreed to end the war and revert to the *status quo ante bellum*. With the Napoleonic wars over and France defeated, impressment was no longer necessary and moreover Britain was exhausted by the European conflict and in no position to wage a long and bloody war to occupy and subdue its former North American colonies.

The United States had survived a war for which it had been unprepared, both militarily and politically. It had failed to take Canada but had advanced the imperial march against Indian lands in the west and south. Tens of thousands of men had served in the US armed forces and militias, with thousands killed by various causes beyond the official casualty figures of 2,260 killed in battle and 4,500 wounded. Once again, the perception of America's destiny and exceptionalism had been affirmed and celebrated by the outcome of a military conflict.

Legislating Ethnic Cleansing

The War of 1812 confirmed American independence and paved the way for the rise of the military hero Jackson, who would orchestrate a massive national campaign of ethnic cleansing of indigenous people. Jackson exalted national pride as well as white supremacy--he was the largest slaveholder in Tennessee—making him one of the most popular presidents in American history. Jackson dominated the exclusively white male vote in three consecutive presidential elections (1824, 1828, 1832) and saw his anointed successor elected in a fourth (Martin Van Buren in 1836).

After defeating and slaughtering both the Red Sticks in Alabama and the British at New Orleans, Jackson had led the US army and militia forces in driving Spain out of Florida. Spain had occupied the peninsula for generations but could no longer hold off the steamroller of American settlement. In 1810 the United States laid claim to so-called West Florida, asserting that it was part of the Louisiana Purchase from France.

Americans resented the Spanish "Dons" for colluding with the Indian tribes as well with "maroons," escaped slaves that southerners viewed as "the vilest species" of humanity. In July 1816 the United States, having constructed Fort Gadsden and other redoubts, attacked the "Negro Fort," where blacks and Indians were holding out on the Apalachicola River in the Florida panhandle. On July 27 a US gunboat fired a red-hot cannonball that struck the fort's magazine, killing scores of people instantly.

In 1818 Jackson razed several indigenous villages, seized a Spanish fort, and summarily hanged two British traders in the process. The Spanish, weakened by the Napoleonic wars and undergoing the dissolution of their

Latin American empire, recognized that they would be unable to hold off the Americans. In 1819 Secretary of State John Quincy Adams negotiated the Transcontinental Treaty in which Spain turned over Florida and moreover became the first European power to recognize an American boundary extending to the Pacific Ocean.

Adams fully grasped the importance of the treaty, which had profound implications. The accord with Spain paved the way for the cleansing campaigns that would now stretch beyond the Rockies and all the way to the Pacific. Ultimately, American imperialism would extend beyond the continent in a quest to control the entire Pacific basin, which would bring on another series of wars in the twentieth century.

In 1824, the House of Representatives decided the contested presidential election in favor of Adams but Jackson, who won the popular vote, denounced the "corrupt bargain" and swamped Adams in the 1828 presidential canvass. The hero president proceeded to carry out his signature policy of Indian Removal, a sweeping and congressionally sanctioned campaign of racially based dispossession throughout the southeastern United States.

The Southeast--which would remain the heartland of American white supremacy for generations--was teeming with black slaves who worked the cotton, rice, and other agricultural fields. The burgeoning British textile mills created high demand for cotton, which also profited the New England shipping industry. Moreover, gold had been discovered on Cherokee land. In sum, Jackson and his fellow southerners decided that the lands were too valuable to let bands of racially inferior Indians retain claim to them.

Masses of Americans, overwhelmingly from north of the Mason-Dixon line, opposed Indian removal, but in the continuous pattern of American history the anti-imperialist forces lost the national debate. Humanitarians and Protestant reformers, fired by a renewed wave of religious revival, the Second Great Awakening, opposed the inhumane treatment of Indians. Many of the same critics denounced the immorality of slavery. Disenfranchisement did not stop American women from spearheading the opposition to Indian dispossession, as they flooded the Congress with anti-removal petitions.

The Indian Removal Act of 1830 overcame the anti-imperialists in part through inclusion of a fraudulent provision in which the United States pledged to remove only "such tribes or nations of Indians as may choose" to vacate their homelands. This pledge was wholly disingenuous, however, as the United States, as it had done in the past and would do in the future, could always induce an Indian faction or avowed leader, depicted as representing the entire tribe, to sign off on the treaty that the whites desired.

In actuality the targeted "five civilized tribes"—Cherokee, Choctaw, Chickasaw, Creek, and Seminole—sharply opposed the dispossession campaign, especially as many of them had acculturated, were the products of mixed marriages, and had converted to Christianity. Some owned prosperous slave plantations themselves. But the white settlers of Mississippi, Alabama, Georgia and other states meant to seize the land mainly to grow cotton.

Jackson and various humanitarians offered the paternalistic argument that the removal campaign was necessary to protect the Indians, who were in any case, as the prominent Kentucky politician Henry Clay put it, an "essentially inferior" as well as a "rapidly disappearing" race. The Cherokee hired attorneys and put up a vigorous defense of their sovereign rights, but the longtime Supreme Court Chief Justice John Marshall sanctioned the cleansing campaign through a series of high court rulings.

The ensuing "trail of tears" was a massive American atrocity, a protracted crime against humanity. Corruption and rampant indifference and inefficiency characterized the removal campaigns, which devolved into a series of death marches. Thousands of Indians perished from exposure, absence of supplies, disease, even a horrific steamboat explosion. The survivors, however, gradually rebuilt their lives and resurrected their cultures in the Oklahoma Territory.

The Americans never did succeed in rooting out all the Indians. The Cherokee--the largest band in the United States today--remained ensconced in pockets of the southeast in the Appalachian Mountains. Infuriating the Americans, including Jackson in his dotage, were the Seminole, who retreated to the Florida swamps and repeatedly fended off US efforts to round up and deport them.

On December 28, 1835, a Seminole band annihilated a US assault force led by Major Francis L. Dade, killing more than 100 men, and virtually wiping out the two army companies. It was the worst defeat suffered at the hands of Indians since the Battle of the Wabash. Two years later Colonel Zachary Taylor amassed a combined force of nearly 400 to attack the Seminole in battle near Lake Okeechobee. Taylor claimed victory but actually lost the battle as the Seminole remained ensconced. "Old Hickory" found no peace in his retirement at the Hermitage, as he fumed over the "disgraceful" and "humiliating" war, insisting that "with fifty women" he could "whip every Indian that had ever crossed the Suwannee."

By 1842 the United States had rounded up and removed some 3,000 Seminole before abandoning the seven-year effort to completely subdue the tribe. About 1,500 Americans and an unknown number of Seminole and their black "maroon" allies died in the counterinsurgency Florida War. A third Seminole War erupted in 1856 and lasted two and a half more years

35

before it too ended inconclusively. The Seminole tribe remains in Florida to this day and proudly proclaims on its web site that it is "the only tribe who never signed a peace treaty."

Indian removal was not limited to the southeast, as the white settlers who continued to flood into the Old Northwest carried out removal campaigns as well. Indians were driven out of Illinois, Wisconsin and Michigan, though a considerable number of Ottawa, Ojibwa and other bands were able to remain in the remote Upper Peninsula of the Wolverine state.

Americans of the day were quick to declare an Indian "uprising" and resort to violence, as in the Black Hawk War, which erupted in 1832 when the eponymous chief of the Sac (Sauk) crossed the Mississippi from the west with a hunting party in search of game needed to survive. Black Hawk proved a capable tactician, as his smaller band of Sac and Fox Indians held off a larger militia force in the Battle of Wisconsin Heights. However, the subsequent "battle" of Bad Axe was actually a massacre in which a large federal force and hundreds of volunteers "needlessly and ruthlessly slaughtered" the tribes and imprisoned Black Hawk. Hundreds of Indians and scores of whites died in the months-long Black Hawk War.

Manifest Destiny—and War

Indian removal underscored that nineteenth century America was a "white man's country" in which Indians, Blacks, Hispanics, and Asians were signified as inferior Others in a cultural process that helped solidify national identity. White supremacy was not confined to the South, as Alexis De Tocqueville and many others observed, but prevailed in the North and the West as well. The ouster of the Spanish, the sweeping campaign of Indian removal, and the expansion of slavery set the stage for the full flowering of Manifest Destiny and a vicious war with Mexico.

At the dawn of the century little was known about the geography, flora and fauna of the trans-Mississippi West, hence Jefferson's decision in the wake of the Louisiana Purchase to dispatch the Corps of Discovery under Meriwether Lewis and William Clark up the Missouri River and on to the Pacific. Both men held military commissions as did subsequent explorers such as Zebulon Pike, Stephen Long and John C. Fremont. The US Army thus played a prominent role in American westward expansion. In 1838 West Point established the Army Topographical Corps to promote mapping and prepare officers for geographic and scientific study as well as warfare. The Army, aided by the reports of fur trappers and skilled guides such as Kit Carson, cleared the path for the masses of American settlers who began to flood into the West on the Santa Fe, Oregon and other trails.

Indigenous people lived throughout the Southwest and California, which the Spanish had attempted to colonize by constructing a dispersed array of missions and fortresses. In 1680 the Pueblo Revolt besieged Spanish colonialism across the southwest. It took 12 years for the Spanish to brutally repress the uprising, but Spain never did succeed in commanding the vast spaces of western North America.

After Mexico won its independence from Spain in 1821, the sparsely settled northern frontier of Texas attracted migrants from the American South. Mexicans and other Latin American nations that won their independence from Spain had been inspired by the US model of republicanism and welcomed US rhetorical support against re-colonization in the Monroe Doctrine (1823). Revolutionaries in Greece, Hungary and other areas of Europe also derived inspiration from the American model in the antebellum years.

Mexicans would find, however, that the war and imperialism intrinsic to American identity overwhelmed the affinities of republicanism. The Mexican Government naively authorized American settlements in Texas on the conditions that the migrants would become citizens and embrace the Catholic Church. These requirements were widely ignored by the Anglo settlers. The Americans in Texas soon outnumbered and viewed themselves as superior to the *Tejanos*, the Hispanic residents of Texas, as well as the myriad Indian tribes in the region.

In 1836 the white migrants declared Texas independence. The Mexican Government sent in the army, which perpetrated massacres at the old Spanish missions of the Alamo and Goliad. The Texans rallied under the Tennessee migrant Sam Houston and crushed General Santa Anna's forces in a surprise attack at San Jacinto. The Texans perpetrated a vengeful massacre, killing 630 to only nine of their own dead in the "battle" of April 21.

The United States tried to buy Texas but Mexico would not sell hence fighting continued. In 1842 Mexican forces retook San Antonio and then were driven out of the city by the Texans in a battle replete with tremendous bloodshed and atrocities. Meanwhile the Texans began gradually to put in place "a policy of ethnic cleansing that had at its intention the forced removal" of Indians and *Tejanos*. The Texas Rangers "killed indiscriminately" and "spread terror so that neighboring Native groups would leave," historian Gary Anderson has recounted.

Texas annexation became a political issue in the 1844 presidential campaign, won by "Young Hickory," James K. Polk, from Jackson's state of Tennessee, who had pledged to bring Texas into the Union whether

Mexico liked it or not. He also demanded that the British vacate the Oregon territory in favor of the Americans.

The full-blown era of Manifest Destiny—a messianic blend of hyper nationalism, evangelical Christianity, and material self-interest--was at hand. Imperialism and war, all sanctioned by God above, were the order of the day.

The United States claimed Texas before Polk took office, but the real prize was California, which would fulfill American destiny not only to dominate North America but moreover to become a Pacific and a world power. Polk thus provoked a war in Texas in order to enable the United States to drive Mexico out of California and New Mexico--a vast territory encompassing the entire southwest, nearly all of today's Nevada and Utah, and extending to the east as far as Nebraska.

The United States provoked the Mexican War by asserting that Texas's boundaries extended south to the Rio Grande—whereas the actual boundary of Texas was well established further north at the Nueces River. By dispatching the Army under now General Taylor into the territory between the two rivers, Polk meant to get the war started. The men under Taylor's command, including Lieutenant Ulysses S. Grant, understood their mission. "We were sent to provoke a fight," Grant noted, "but it was essential that Mexico should commence it." When Mexican and American forces duly clashed on April 25, 1846, Polk mendaciously declared that Mexico had "shed American blood on American soil," that a state of war thus existed "by act of Mexico" despite "all our acts to avoid it."

It would not be the last time an American president lied and manufactured evidence to justify a war that he wanted to initiate. Feverish with Manifest Destiny, the Congress declared war by votes of 174-14 in the House and 40-2 in the Senate.

In addition to its crusading zeal, the United States had a larger population, a 50-year head start on republican government, and much greater wealth and power than the disconnected, sprawling and still developing Mexican state. Moreover, residents of the areas targeted by the North Americans—*Tejanos*, *Californios*, and *Nuevomexicanos*—were deeply frustrated with the far-off central government in Mexico City, which provided few services and had proven unable to protect vulnerable residents from the scourge of raiding Indian bands. Polk and his military advisers recognized and meant to capitalize on the situation in which the relentless attacks by the Comanche, Kiowa and other tribes had weakened Mexico's ability to resist a Yankee invasion on the northern and southwestern borderlands.

The United States might have been able to capitalize on the widespread disenchantment in which many Mexicans on the periphery would welcome US sovereignty, but the toxic racism and indiscriminate war carried out by the American volunteers quickly ended any hope of such an outcome. As a result of these factors, Mexican popular resistance proved much stiffer and more sustained than Americans expected, making for a long and ugly imperial conflict.

Americans retained their republican suspicions of large standing armies and thus relied on the volunteers, venerated by Polk as "free citizens, who are ever ready to take up arms in the service of their country when an emergency requires it." The US military of the era thus maintained a shell Army that it could fill out in time of war with volunteers. Congress appropriated $10 million to raise the Army ranks to 15,540 augmented by 50,000 volunteers. As the war unfolded, it became clear that the Army did not have the organization and cohesion to effectively command the undisciplined and often bloodthirsty volunteers. The consequences of this reality would be devastating—especially for the Mexican people.

In May 1846 Taylor's forces overcame Mexican resistance at the border city of Matamoros, at which point the volunteers descended upon the town with pistols and Bowie knives to rob, rape, and murder its residents. Men had been primed in advance, as "the propaganda surrounding the war was nakedly opportunistic and expressly promised plunder as the right of the volunteer," as historian Paul Foos has explained. With Mexico widely depicted as a "barbarous Catholic country," the volunteers tore down churches and savaged priests and nuns.

Taylor recognized that the violent actions of the volunteers were undermining the American strategy to win quick military victories and convince Mexico to give up resistance in favor of peace negotiations. "No more effectual plan could be devised to rouse the Mexican people to resistance than the very one pursued by some of our volunteer regiments," Taylor lamented. "There is scarcely a form of crime that has not been reported to me as committed by them."

In the first months of the war the United States thus alienated the bulk of the Mexican population, many of which had been deeply frustrated with their own government and might have been amenable to acquiescing to a disciplined occupation. Many of these Mexican citizens had expected a dramatically different approach from a sister republic and were shocked by the violent depravity of the American assault and occupation policies. With nothing to lose in the face of the widespread robbery, murder and sexual assault by the US forces, Mexicans took up a guerrilla resistance characterized by sniping, sabotage, and hit and run attacks.

Advancing to Monterey, Taylor encountered entrenched regular Mexican Army forces who mounted a determined resistance. After American howitzers shelled the citadel, fierce house-to-house fighting culminated in the surrender of the city in September. As a two-year occupation, the longest of any Mexican city, began, Taylor again failed to establish security patrols thus enabling the volunteers to run amok. Lieutenant Daniel H. Hill expressed the disgust of many regulars as he noted the "beastly depravity and gross outrages of the volunteers" against the defenseless residents of Monterey.

The worst offenders were the Texas Rangers, who carried out brutal assaults that made the Mexicans "dread the Texans more than they do the devil," as one soldier put it. "The mounted men from Texas have scarcely made one expedition without unwarrantably killing a Mexican," Taylor acknowledged, but other volunteer groups, such as the "Rackensackers" from Arkansas, carried out well chronicled mass murders and depredations as well.

Although he condemned the undisciplined volunteers Taylor failed to rein them in and conducted a scorched-earth campaign of his own in response to the sniping and guerrilla resistance. He authorized collective punishment and burning of villages. These actions only further embittered and intensified Mexican resistance.

While Taylor and the volunteers laid waste to northern Mexico, General Stephen Watts Kearny assembled 300 Army dragoons accompanied by 1,000 Missouri volunteer mounted infantry for a march from Fort Leavenworth to Santa Fe. By the time they arrived in August, several men and horses had died from heat-related causes.

Kearny encountered no resistance in Santa Fe, as again many of the residents of the Mexican frontier were open to American sovereignty in part because they had received no protection from the central government from Indian depredations. Kearny set up a provincial government and wrote a new constitution but quickly alienated the *Nuevomexicanos* by placing US merchants in charge of economic affairs, which they dominated to the detriment of the local residents. In January 1847 an angry mob of impoverished pueblo Indians and Hispanics murdered Governor Charles Bent at his home in Taos while his wife and children narrowly escaped. A volunteer force eventually responded by riding into town and massacring 150 people to only seven of its own killed.

In California, Hispanic elites like Mariano Vallejo welcomed the arrival of Major John C. Fremont, guided by Kit Carson, as they launched the "Bear Flag Revolt" to detach California from Mexico in June 1846. Vallejo and other local Hispanics had long expressed frustration with the distant government in Mexico City, but Fremont and US Navy Commodore Robert Stockton, arriving by sea, quickly alienated the locals with racist disdain, including arbitrary arrest and imprisonment of Vallejo and some other *Californios*. Arriving with a small force in southern California, Kearny suffered a defeat in battle but was bailed out by Stockton's Marines, who had seized San Diego. In January 1847 the combined US forces took the small town of Los Angeles.

Having defeated Mexico on every front, all that remained was for the Mexican government to sign a peace treaty that would provide diplomatic sanction to Yankee imperialism and bring a halt to the guerrilla resistance. But Mexicans were deeply embittered over the affronts to their dignity and the rampant atrocities of the volunteers. When the Mexican government refused his demands, Polk ordered a march on Mexico City.

Much like Taylor, General Winfield Scott, put in charge of the campaign, was appalled by US atrocities in the conflict. "Our militia and volunteers," he acknowledged, "if a tenth of what is said to be true, have committed atrocities—horrors—in Mexico, sufficient to make Heaven weep." Scott meant to crack down on the "unchristian and cruel" war crimes by reining in liquor sales and establishing commissions to investigate alleged perpetrators. He hanged at least one rapist, but military justice did not extend to the civilian volunteers, the worst offenders, who had the right to be tried in civilian courts, where their fellow white male citizens back in the States had little interest in punishing assaults on Mexicans.

Scott's sympathies for the Mexican people quickly waned, as in March 1847 he unleashed an indiscriminate bombardment of the port city of Vera Cruz, killing some 400 civilians along with about 350 soldiers. "My heart bled for the inhabitants," Captain Robert E. Lee, who engineered the bombardment, told his wife.

The Mexicans surrendered Vera Cruz but maintained a guerrilla resistance, which prompted Scott to authorize summary executions and collective punishment destroying entire towns. The Mexicans had every reason to believe the Americans would kill them no matter what and thus many preferred to go down fighting. General Santa Anna condemned any negotiations with the invaders. As Scott began the march on Mexico City, a newspaper in the capital declared that the Americans intended to "burn our cities, loot our temples, rape our wives and daughters, and kill our sons."

In September, Scott's army took the city after a bloody fight culminating in the surrender of Chapultepec castle. Santa Anna fled, Scott declared martial law, and another atrocious occupation ensued. Hill, the future Confederate general, described US forces as "fearfully corrupted" and "perfectly frantic with lust for blood and plunder." Other observers noted that troops "maddened with liquor" carried out "every species of outrage" on the Mexican occupants.

While Polk grew frustrated over Mexico's intransigence and fell out with the chief American diplomat Nicholas Trist, as well as with Scott, much of public, still feverish with Manifest Destiny, called for the incorporation into the Union of "all Mexico." However, by this time a vocal opposition had materialized against "Mr. Polk's War" and the "wicked war," which Whig politicians and some others viewed as part of a southern plot to permanently ensconce slavery. New England transcendentalists condemned US aggression as well as the nation's rampant materialism, but they were a distinct minority of marginalized New England intellectuals. As throughout American history, anti-imperial sentiment had failed to preclude the waging of an aggressive war.

In 1848 Trist and Mexican elites mercifully concluded the Treaty of Guadalupe-Hidalgo bringing an end to the inglorious conflict. The United States paid Mexico $15 million for the massive imperial land grab, augmented six years later by another $10 million for the coerced Gadsden Purchase, which the Americans demanded to facilitate construction of the southern route of the transcontinental railroad. Nearly 14,000 Americans died in the Mexican War, the overwhelming majority of those from disease and other non-combat causes. At least 25,000 Mexicans died in the war. The war had cost the United States about $100 million.

While taking the war aggressively to Mexico, Polk backed off when threatened with British military power over his demand for drawing an Oregon boundary at the 54th parallel of north latitude. In the Oregon Treaty of 1846, the Americans settled for the current boundary at the 49th parallel. Whereas they had been eager for war with the brown-skinned "mongrel" and Catholic Mexicans, the Americans settled diplomatically with their fellow white imperial and Protestant Britons.

By the mid-nineteenth century, in the wake of Manifest Destiny, imperialism and war were thoroughly ensconced in the DNA of American national identity. A decade later the nation's penchant for violent aggression would blow back in monumental fashion on the United States itself.

Chapter 3
Uncivil War and Imperialism

In the Civil War (1861-1865), American violence turned inward, with devastating consequences. The internecine conflict was an example of unforeseen consequences and blowback from a previous war. What appeared to be a great national triumph of Manifest Destiny instead sowed the seeds of an incomparably destructive war.

Because of slavery and the unresolved constitutional conflict between states' rights and federalism, the United States could not politically digest the vast swath of new territory taken from Mexico and the Indians. The political system began to break down immediately after the Mexican War, was propped up by an ephemeral compromise, and ultimately collapsed into the depths of virulent civil tumult.

More than anything else, of course, the reactionary institution of slavery, which nearly every other nation in the world had abandoned by 1861, brought on the Civil War. With its in many ways ingenious Constitution and robust republican institutions, the United States was in some respects arguably the most progressive nation in the world. Along with the French Revolution, the Americans had helped inspire republican experiments throughout the world. Yet in other ways, especially through the entrenchment and vigorous defense of slavery, the United States was also one of the most retrograde countries in the world. Indeed, the dialectic between freedom and repression, goes to the very heart and soul of American history.

Ironically, the intensity of American exceptionalism caused the Civil War. Pro-Union forces rejected the Confederate argument that the states had joined the Union willingly and could leave it the same way. The Civil War, as the speeches and veritable poetry of Abraham Lincoln at Gettysburg and elsewhere made clear, was a war to preserve the American union of states, "the last best hope of earth," as Lincoln declaimed.

The Civil War became a blood-drenched modern war, pitting mass armies against one another on a series of sprawling battlefields, but it would also devolve into a bitter guerrilla war replete with localized indiscriminate killing and collective punishment. By the time it was over, scholars now estimate the number of dead at 750,000, making it by far the most violent conflict in American history.

Following the election in 1860, which brought into power the anti-slavery—which is not to say abolitionist—Republican Party, with Lincoln of Illinois at the head of the ticket, the cotton states seceded. In April 1861 fighting erupted over the status of the small federal installation off the South Carolina coast. The bombardment forced the Union to surrender Fort Sumter in a clash that galvanized pro-war sentiment on both sides, including the critical decision of the states of the Upper South to secede.

Much like the First World War more than a half century in the future, the belligerents were blissfully ignorant of the potential scope and carnage of the conflict that they were unleashing. The principles of modern warfare had been applied to some extent in the Mexican War as well as the Crimean War (1853-56), but they would play out on a massive scale in the Civil War. By 1860 more than 75 percent of US Army officers—men who would wage war on both sides in the Civil War—had graduated from West Point, where they had studied the revolutionary changes flowing out of the Napoleonic wars (1803-15). Napoleon had amassed a huge army and emphasized the overwhelming use of force combined with maneuverability, including mobile artillery. He also proved willing to absorb and inflict mass casualties. Following the Napoleonic wars, the Frenchman Antoine Henri Jomini analyzed modern warfare in published studies emphasizing the role of strategy, the importance of taking the initiative, forcing the opponent to react, and finding weaknesses, all of which entered into the West Point curriculum.

Another brilliant student of war, the Prussian theorist Karl von Clausewitz probed the essence of war, not an end in itself but a means to the end of compelling political change. Clausewitz also emphasized the contingency and unpredictability of war—decision-making and consequential actions would be taken within a "fog of war"—hence matters invariably would not go as planned and might well go awry.

New technology made the Civil War more deadly than any previous war. Both armies wreaked havoc with mobile 12-pound cannon for long-range artillery. The Sharps carbine and Spencer repeating rifles were far more accurate and deadly than outmoded muzzle-loading muskets.

General Winfield Scott, the grizzled veteran of wars dating to 1812, developed the Union strategy, known as the Anaconda Plan, which envisioned blockading the Confederacy by sea, taking control of the Mississippi River and gradually squeezing the life out of the rebellion. The Union had clear advantages of a larger population, far more capacity for industrial output than the traditional southern agrarian society, as well as an expansive rail network and telegraph lines for movement of troops and supplies and rapid communications. The Confederacy had one advantage but it was formidable—it would have to be occupied and conquered in order to be defeated.

Both sides deployed masses of volunteers but also instituted conscription as they assembled armies comprised of infantry, artillery and cavalry. Exemptions were granted in both North and South, enabling elites to avoid the war if they chose. Masses of men resisted conscription on both sides, but especially in the North, where the draft provoked the largest rioting in American history in New York City in July 1863.

The Civil War brought a sharp erosion of civil liberties. Of course, even before the war free speech had been deeply compromised over much of the South, as anyone advocating abolition of slavery would be tarred and feathered, at best. Once the war began, the Union also cracked down on dissent. Lincoln authorized military tribunals and suspended habeas corpus and due process for opponents of the draft or the war. The Union censored the press, arrested editors, shut down newspapers and equated free speech critical of Union actions or calling for an end to the bloodshed with disloyalty and treason. Wrestling with whether the government would be "too strong for the liberties of its own people, or too weak to maintain its own existence," Lincoln came down firmly on the side of avoiding the latter.

After a series of bloody conflicts, the pivotal Battle of Antietam near Sharpsburg, Maryland turned the tide of the war, but more for the political reasons assessed by Clausewitz than for military victory, as the battle was essentially a draw. To this day September 17, 1862 remains the bloodiest day in American history as the clash of the two mass armies left a sprawling cornfield, the "Bloody Lane," and "Burnside's Bridge" littered with dead, totaling some 3,650 with more than 17,000 wounded.

Lincoln, more gifted as a political than a military leader, seized the opportunity to issue the Emancipation Proclamation, declaring that slaves in the rebel states (but not the border states) were freed. The Emancipation ennobled the war, made it increasingly a fight for human freedom, affirming support north of the Mason-Dixon line and eliminating the prospect of foreign intervention, as neither Britain nor France could embrace a war for the continuation of slavery. Southern efforts to exploit the British textile industry's reliance on "king cotton" as a diplomatic weapon failed, in part because Britain tapped Egypt for stepped up cotton imports.

The Civil War became a modern "total war" featuring a series of well-known set battles with high casualty rates, but less well known it also became a brutal guerrilla and counterinsurgency war as well. The American Civil War, often romanticized as a noble war among honorable men, in actuality, as a few scholars have pointed out, was a "savage conflict" characterized by rage-filled and indiscriminate killing and atrocities reminiscent of the Mexican and Indian wars.

In 1862 the Confederacy passed the Partisan Ranger Act unleashing irregular warfare and indiscriminate killing. Some of the most atrocious irregular warfare occurred in Missouri, a border state that remained in the Union but where pro-Rebel sympathies had been pronounced since the era of "bleeding Kansas" preceding the war. Guerrilla leaders such as William Quantrill and "Bloody Bill" Anderson led astonishingly violent campaigns replete with mass murder and mutilation. Arkansas, Kentucky, Tennessee, and Texas were also the sites of brutal guerrilla conflict.

In order to subdue the South, the Union took up counterinsurgency warfare well before General William Tecumseh Sherman's famous march to the sea. The Yankees responded to guerrilla assaults with summary executions and collective punishment, as they plundered and put to the torch farms, towns, and whole cities. Following decisive victories at Gettysburg and Vicksburg in the summer of 1863, the Union forces methodically drove Old Dixie down.

The sectional hatreds would not soon abate, greatly complicating the effort at postwar Reconstruction following Lee's surrender at Appomattox Courthouse, Virginia. Roiled by the assassination of Lincoln and the impeachment of his successor, Andrew Johnson, the Union struggled for consensus on a policy to reintegrate the defeated rebel states.

The war was over, but the deep-seated culture of white supremacy remained entrenched. The promise of the 13th, 14th, and 15th amendments thus went unrealized in the South, which was "redeemed" in a process that culminated with the Compromise of 1877 in the wake of the disputed 1876 presidential election. Reconstruction ended in failure.

It would take decades for the United States to rebuild national unity out of the profound sectional divisions that had spawned the Civil War. Yet ultimately the defeat of the Confederacy transformed the United States into a modern nation rather than a mere grouping of states.

Crucial to recovery and revitalization of the Union was the revival of national imperialism. Americans of north and south found common ground behind completing the national imperial project of subjugating and removing Indians from the land to make way for millions of migrating white settlers. Imperialism and war—fulfilling the promise of Manifest Destiny—thus served to heal the wound within.

"Winning the West"

Masses of Indians west of the Mississippi River posed the final challenge to the establishment of a hegemonic state spanning the continent. Under the Indian Removal Act (1830) the United States had promised to "forever secure and guarantee" the new "Indian country" that stretched from the Oklahoma territory across the Great Plains to modern day Montana. Jackson's Secretary of War Lewis Cass had offered the "solemn promise" that this vast new territory would be "reserved for the red people; it will be yours as long as the sun shines and the rain falls."

American settlers, however, were already by the 1830s cutting a swath through Indian country on the Oregon Trail and discovering that an agricultural heartland rather than the long presumed "great American desert" appeared before them. In the wake of the Mexican War and Kansas-Nebraska Act (1854), there was little doubt that once again Indians would be removed from the land. The "Indian barrier . . . filled with hostile savages" must give way to farms, towns, railroads, and commerce, the Illinois Senator Stephen A. Douglas declared.

In the continuous pattern of American imperialism, Indians would be removed from desired land--by treaty if possible, by force replete with massacre if deemed necessary. In some places the speed and scope of the indigenous removal project accelerated into genocide.

Throughout this process as in earlier periods of history some indigenous bands entered alliances with US forces or served as scouts in campaigns against other tribes, but rarely did such cooperation produce a favorable outcome for Indians.

As a result of the 1849 Gold Rush, American settlement leapfrogged the Rocky Mountains to the Pacific Coast. The Gold Rush spurred a mad dash to California, including thousands of Chinese immigrants who sought to settle in the American Far West. Many of the Asian migrants undertook the most thankless work of hard-rock mining and railroad construction through the perilous passes of the Rockies and the High Sierras.

Under the dictates of imperial white supremacy, the Chinese as well as Blacks, Hispanics and Indians were not accorded legitimacy in American society. Over the last half of the nineteenth century white Western American settlers targeted Chinese migrants in hundreds of ethnic cleansing operations, uprooting communities, seizing property, and slaughtering them. "As with Indians to whom whites often compared the Chinese, the way such killings were carried out revealed a deep, almost feral hatred," historian David Courtwright has noted. "Chinese men were scalped, mutilated, burned, branded, decapitated, dismembered, and hanged from gutter spouts." In 1882--as with Indian removal a half century before--the Congress made the cleansing campaign a national policy, as the Chinese Exclusion Act cut off Chinese immigration into the United States.

Settlers perpetrated an even more concerted homicidal rampage—indeed, an outright genocide—against the indigenous people of California. As the settler population catapulted in the wake of the Gold Rush from 92,000 in 1851 to 380,000 by 1860, California settlers slaughtered Indians before the Army or federal authorities could respond or put into effect an Indian policy. In 1851 Governor Peter Burnet sanctioned what he called a "a war of extermination . . . until the Indian race becomes extinct." Thousands were slaughtered and others sold into servitude.

Across California disease took a heavy toll on Indians but at the same time land-hungry settlers and their militias murdered thousands of Native Americans and enslaved thousands of others. The Army occupied California after the Mexican War but did nothing to stop the slaughter. An Army major acknowledged that the settlers had carried out a "relentless war of extermination . . . They have ruthlessly massacred men, women, and children." A California newspaper rationalized, "Extermination is the cheapest and quickest remedy" for the Indian problem.

While Far Western settlers killed Indians indiscriminately, indigenous massacres of white settlers were far less prevalent than post-World War II Hollywood Westerns would later suggest. Indian attacks on settler wagon trains streaming West were rare. In fact, the largest attack on a wagon train, at Mountain Meadows in the Utah territory in 1857, was perpetrated by Mormon settlers on other trekkers rather than by free-roaming Indians.

On the Oregon Trail, more settlers died from drowning than Indian attack, yet episodic attacks did occur. In the 1854 Ward massacre, for example, Shoshone Indians killed and mutilated 19 migrants from Missouri about 25 miles east of Fort Boise. Outcries from settlers prompted more patrolling from the Army, which in January 1863 perpetrated one of the worst massacres of Indians in US history on the Bear River near the Utah-Idaho border. Under Colonel Patrick Conner, the troops went on an undisciplined rampage killing at least 224 Indians, and perhaps more than twice that number, while also perpetrating rapes and mutilation.

At this same time the Five Civilized Tribes that had been forcibly removed to the Oklahoma Territory were caught up in the maelstrom of the Civil War. Since the 1830s the Cherokee, Choctaw, Chickasaw, Creek and Seminole had rebuilt their lives, though often in conflict with the culturally divergent Plains tribes that already lived in the area. As the Civil War spilled over into Indian country, the Choctaw and Chickasaw sided with the Confederacy while the other three tribes were divided in their loyalties. The conflict destroyed the entire social fabric—towns, churches, schools—within the Oklahoma Indian communities.

By the end of the Civil War, some 20,000 US Army troops were serving in the West and thus positioned to cleanse Indians from the land to make way for homesteaders who were propelled west by the offer of virtually free land under the 1862 Homestead Act. Little better underscored the realities of American imperialism than the offer of free land to white settlers while taking ground away from the indigenous people. Miners, cattlemen, railroad construction, cities and factories quickly flourished west of the Mississippi.

Westerners had no patience with Eastern humanitarians who attempted to argue the Indians' case. Pressured by humanitarians, the newly elected President Grant in 1869 trumpeted his "peace policy," which entailed forcing Indians off the land and onto reservations where they could receive assistance and the blessings of civilization. If they refused to abandon their culture and homeland, however, Grant promised they would be met with "a sharp and severe war policy."

The US Army chafed over the placement of the Bureau of Indian Affairs under the Department of the Interior rather than the War Department, but the military men did not let government bureaucracy impede them. After the Civil War, the War Department gave General Sherman command over a vast space from St. Louis to the Continental Divide, which he meant to rid of "free roaming" Indians. While acknowledging that "grievous wrong" had been done to the indigenous people, Sherman resolved to remove them from the path of settlement. Should they resist, Sherman vowed to destroy the tribes by waging the style of warfare with which he was well acquainted.

Another relentless Union general, Philip Sheridan, adopted the same approach to the indigenous "miserable wretches." Sheridan--like many military men on the "frontier," but much less famously than, say, Japanese soldiers in World War II--enjoyed the services of an Indian concubine. Yet Sheridan once proclaimed that the only good Indian was a dead one. Enraged whenever Indians attacked settlers or resisted US directives, Sherman and Sheridan would respond with exterminatory rhetoric and the attendant military policies.

In November 1864, with Army Colonel John Chivington at the head of a volunteer force, the Americans perpetrated one of the most perfidious massacres in US history at Sand Creek in the Colorado territory. The Cheyenne under the leadership of Black Kettle had encamped along the creek in the eastern Plains portion of the territory with the permission of Colorado authorities, but the governor nonetheless authorized the murderous surprise attack directed by Chivington, a fanatical Methodist minister and head of the Colorado militia. The marauders killed some 230 innocent Cheyenne and Arapaho men, women, and children. The Army and a federal commission condemned the "gross and wanton outrages" committed at Sand Creek, but as always there would be no punishment merely for killing Indians. The territorial governor, John Evans, justified the genocidal assault explaining, "The benefit to Colorado of that massacre, as they call it, was very great for it ridded the plains of the Indians."

Unlike Black Kettle, some of the younger Cheyenne warriors, known as the "dog soldiers," continued to resist and attack white settlements, prompting Sherman to go into a rage and declare, "Now this must come to a violent end." He authorized Lieutenant Colonel George Armstrong Custer, one of the heroes of Gettysburg (and like Sheridan an Army man who kept an Indian mistress), to attack the Cheyenne, who had removed to an encampment along the Washita River near the Texas Panhandle-Oklahoma border.

As the accompanying regimental band played a jolly Irish folk tune, Custer attacked at dawn on November 26, 1868, killing more than 100 Indians, including Black Kettle, destroying tepees and food stores, and slaughtering some 700 horses and ponies in order to deprive the tribe of mobility. As Indians who were encamped downriver rallied to the fight, Custer beat a hasty retreat abandoning a column of soldiers who as a result were surrounded, killed, and mutilated.

The Civil War had enabled the powerful Comanche as well as the Kiowa and other Plains tribes to step up their raiding in Texas but following the war the Texas Rangers resumed the offensive. They attacked Comanche villages, slaughtering men, women, and children by the hundreds.

The Army took up the attack on the Plains tribes in the 1870s in a series of clashes known as the Red River Wars. The Army simultaneously encouraged the slaughter of the bison, with Sheridan asserting in 1875 that buffalo hunters, by "destroying the Indians' commissary," had "done more in the last two years to settle the vexed Indian question than the regular army has done in the past thirty years."

The Red River campaign ended in September when the Army drove the Comanche, Kiowa, and remaining Cheyenne from Palo Duro Canyon, burning villages and slaughtering some 1,000 horses in the process. Bereft of food and shelter, Indians had little choice but to file onto the reservation. By 1875 only a few thousand Indians remained in Texas, where an estimated 35,000 had roamed freely in 1835.

Following the Civil War, "The bulldozer of American removal hit the Rockies hard," as historian Ned Blackhawk explains, "scaling the nation's tallest peaks and descending into mountain valleys in search of the next Native community to uproot." Although the Ute had assisted the Army in an assault on the Navaho, it had also clashed with cattlemen in Colorado's San Luis valley as well as Mormon settlers in Utah. Sherman ordered the Ute driven from their Rocky Mountain homeland onto a reservation in the new territory named for them.

From 1864 to 1868 the Hopi and Zuni tribes had joined the Ute in assisting the Army in the campaign against the Navaho, who had clashed with settlers and attacked the American outpost of Fort Defiance in the

Arizona Territory. Made an Army Lieutenant Colonel and dispatched to the southwest during the Civil War, Kit Carson led the scorched-earth assault on the Navaho homeland of Canyon de Chelly.

The Navaho who survived Carson's attack were sent on the "long walk" to a barren encampment in New Mexico--a death march far less well known but equally as infamous as the one the Japanese forced on Americans at Bataan in World War II. The Army killed Indians, including pregnant women and children, who could not keep pace, and others died after arriving at the inhospitable new site, where the water was barely potable. Seizing, however, upon the ephemerally more favorable outlook toward Indians fostered by the "peace policy," Navaho leaders in Washington skillfully negotiated a return to Canyon de Chelly, where they remain to this day as the second most populous tribe (behind the Cherokee) in the United States.

In the Arizona territory settlers clashed with the Apache, including the Chiricahua band led by Cochise. In 1861 the Army killed Cochise's wife and some of his children, prompting him to go on the warpath for the next decade until a peace treaty took him into retirement on a reservation. Hundreds of Apache did not escape with their lives, as the Arizonans carried out a genocidal rampage wherein "Indians are shot wherever seen," as envoys advised President Lincoln, including even those who retreated to the reservations.

In the infamous Camp Grant massacre, perpetrated on April 30, 1871, settlers led a group of Mexicans and Papago Indians in a dawn attack slaughtering 108 peacefully encamped Apache in Aravaipa Canyon some 60 miles northeast of Tucson. The Army condemned the attack as "but another massacre, in cold blood, of inoffensive and peaceful Indians who were living on the reservation under the protection of the Government," but settlers, the regional press, and political leaders celebrated the event. The massacre was "one of the most important victories ever achieved by the white men over the savages of Arizona," a newspaper proclaimed, adding its endorsement of "extermination of the Apaches."

A small band of Chiricahua led by Geronimo eluded the Army for years in the Arizona deserts and mountains, finally negotiating a surrender in 1886. The Army eventually lodged Geronimo at Fort Sill, Oklahoma, where he died and was buried. In 1918 members of Yale's Skull and Bones fraternal society, including Prescott Bush, the patriarch of two future US presidents, looted the grave as a prank. Despite being on a US army base, the grave site continues to be subjected to periodic desecration.

Also skillfully eluding the Army was Chief Joseph, leader of the Nez Perce Indians in the American Northwest. As in California, attacks on Indians began early and often in the Oregon Territory around the time of the treaty with Great Britain (1846). In that year the ubiquitous Carson led a slaughter of Klamath Indians—whom he had mistakenly blamed for an attack on his camp—commenting on the "beautiful sight" as the Indian village burned to the ground.

Indian killing in Oregon accelerated the following year after the murder of 14 Americans by the Cayuse band. The dead included the Presbyterian missionary couple Marcus and Narcissa Whitman. The pair had traveled to Oregon to save Indians' souls but ended up detesting them. The feeling was mutual.

Oregon settlers seized on the Whitman and other killings to launch exterminatory campaigns against the Cayuse, Klamath, Yakima, Chinooks and other tribes. In 1855 Isaac Stevens, Oregon's first territorial governor and head of the Pacific Railroad Survey, called for "extermination," promising a Yakima chief in Walla Walla, "If you do not accept the terms offered, you will walk in blood knee deep."

The Nez Perce, who had peaceful relations with Americans since the time of Lewis and Clark, allied with the settlers against other tribes in the Yakima War (1855-58). The alliance enabled the Nez Perce to maintain their homeland for another generation, but by the 1870s encroaching settlement led to a clash that included killings and rapes of white women by the previously peaceful tribe. Led by Joseph the Nez Perce alternately successfully engaged and eluded the US Army for weeks, killing a few tourists in the new Yellowstone Park in the process. The Nez Perce traversed Montana and nearly made it across the border into Canada. Finally captured, Chief Joseph told General Nelson Miles, "I will fight no more." He later claimed to have converted to Christianity, which he used to lobby successfully for the Nez Perce to escape confinement in Kansas and receive a reservation in Idaho.

The grouping of tribes known as the Sioux mounted the most potent resistance to American imperialism. In August 1862, deeply frustrated over the depletion of resources and erosion of their Minnesota hunting grounds, the Santee Sioux launched a genocidal uprising against the mostly German settlers. Before it was over the Santee slaughtered 400-600 Minnesotans as well as 140 soldiers in the largest Indian massacre of settlers in all of American history. The Army finally quelled the uprising and executed 38 Indians on December 26. It was the largest mass execution in US history, but the number would have been far greater had not Lincoln commuted the death sentences of 265 Indians.

The Army rampaged across the northern plains in the wake of the Sioux uprising, driving the band into the Dakota territory. There the Sioux clashed with other tribes and with Americans trekking to Oregon. In 1851 the Sioux signed a treaty with the United States pledging to tolerate the migrants in return for annuities. Three years later, however, after being confronted by John L. Grattan, a hot-headed young lieutenant, a group of Sioux killed 30 men at the trading post at Fort Laramie.

The clash ignited the First Sioux War, which led to the slaughter of at least 86 Sioux, more than half non-combatant women and children, at Blue Water Creek in Nebraska. The Army took Sioux captives and began methodically to surround the Sioux homelands with new forts. In December 1866, the Sioux, led by the aggressive young warrior Crazy Horse, perpetrated the "Fetterman massacre," wiping out a force of 80 troopers led by Captain William Fetterman, who had been lured into an ambush beyond Fort Phil Kearny in the Powder River country.

The Fetterman killings provoked an episodic burst of rage from Sherman, who vowed to carry the war "with vindictiveness earnestness against the Sioux, even to their extermination, men, women, and children." The Oglala Sioux leader Red Cloud, however, forged a second Fort Laramie Treaty in 1868 under which the Sioux pledged to bury the hatchet in return for the promise that they could keep in perpetuity as their reservation the Black Hills region in today's western South Dakota. Within a few years, however, railroad interests and the discovery of gold in the Black Hills prompted the United States to renege on the treaty.

Dispatched to the region at the head of the 7th Cavalry, now General Custer was charged with scouting sites for a new fort and confirming the existence of gold in the Black Hills, but as always, the aggressive commander was looking for a fight through which he could claim glory. Riding with Custer were Crow warriors, inveterate enemies of the rival Sioux. As Custer like Fetterman wandered deep into Indian country, the Crow scouts tried to warn him, but the golden-haired hero—much like General Braddock in 1754--did not believe Indians capable of mobilizing an army large enough to challenge him. Just a week earlier, however, the Lakota chief Sitting Bull together with Crazy Horse had bested General George Crook and his Crow and Shoshone allies at the Battle of Rosebud on June 17, 1876.

Custer compounded his underestimation of the tribes by dividing his regiment. He was thus badly outnumbered as he entered the valley of Little Big Horn Creek—the Indians called it the Greasy Grass—where he encountered a war-painted army of some 2,000 Sioux, Northern Cheyenne and Arapaho. On June 25 the Indians savaged the 7th Cavalry, killing 268 troopers, including Custer, who was later found mutilated on the battlefield. It was the largest defeat suffered by the US Army in Indian conflict since the 1791 Battle of the Wabash in western Ohio. But as in that case, the Indian victory was ephemeral, as the Sioux and their allies were soon outnumbered, surrounded and forced onto reservations.

As the Army and settlers subjugated the tribes, demands increased for greater efforts to assimilate Indians into American life. Humanitarian critics had kept up a steady drumbeat against a punitive, militarized policy toward indigenous people. In 1881 one such marginalized critic, Helen Hunt Jackson, published the bestseller *A Century of Dishonor*, which chronicled and condemned a long history of American injustice toward Indians.

Under the consensus framework of American national identity, ethnic cleansing and by now Social Darwinism prevailed over anti-imperialism. As in the War of 1812 and the Mexican War, dissenters were limited primarily to the northeast and made little impact on the actual removal process across the mountains and plains of the American West. Moreover, most "humanitarian" critics deplored the violence rather than the concept of Indian removal and were thus themselves imperialists who shared the American consensus that Indians should be removed and "saved" by being forced to adopt a superior white culture.

In 1887 the assimilationist movement culminated with a colonial solution embodied by the Dawes Act, which subdivided reservation land into 160-acre plots while at the same time opening up yet more Indian land for white settlement. By this time the United States had begun to remove Indian children from their homes, which today would be considered a war crime, and to transport them back East where they could be civilized and reprogrammed out of their indigenous identities. In 1879 an abandoned military base at Carlisle, Pennsylvania, directed by Army General Richard Henry Pratt, became the prototypical "school of savages." The school pursued a figurative "kill the Indian, save the man" program of reeducation, but in the early years of its operation more Indians died of disease than graduated.

Various Indian bands adapted and acculturated as best they could in the midst of the imperial onslaught while striving desperately to retain their "Indianness." As a Dakota land boom evolved, forging the creation of separate North and South Dakota states, settlers carved more land out of the Sioux reservations. At this time, the spiritually inspired Ghost Dance, through which Indians imagined the return of the bison, disappearance of the white man, and thus the revival of their cultures and prosperity spread across the reservations.

As panicky settlers expressed groundless fears of an Indian uprising, the Army overreacted as it dispatched to the Dakotas the largest force sent anywhere since the Civil War. Tensions were high, especially when the legendary leader Sitting Bull was ripped out of his sleep and killed along with one of his sons at the Standing Rock Reservation.

On December 15, 1890, a rifle shot at the Pine Ridge Reservation incited jittery soldiers who according to an on-the-scene report "began shooting in every direction, killing not only Indians but also their own comrades." The US troops then began slaughtering Indians, including deployment of five-barrel Hotchkiss guns that "sent a storm of shells . . . mowing down everything alive." Some 150 Indians were killed that day and another 100 as the killing went on for days. Twenty-five troopers died, mostly from friendly fire. Absurdly, the United States awarded 18 Congressional Medals of Honor, ostensibly for bravery in "battle."

Just as absurdly, General Miles claimed to have prevented a "wild, mad horde of savages" from launching an uprising. Sherman, by then a septuagenarian, cheered on the slaughter, explaining that the more Miles "kills now, the less he will have to do later." Episodic skirmishes played out over the next few years, but for the most part centuries of American Indian wars were over, fittingly punctuated by a massacre of people held captive on land the United States had pledged by treaty was to have remained theirs in perpetuity.

Chapter 4
Globalizing Imperialism and War

As it carried out the prolonged campaign of continental ethnic cleansing after the Civil War, the United States simultaneously became a modern industrial nation. By the turn of the century the Americans had burst had onto the world stage with imperial thrusts and warfare stretching from the Caribbean Sea across the Pacific and into Southeast Asia.

The massive Union war effort included federal sponsorship of railroad construction, igniting the dominant industry of the postwar Industrial Era. The railroad age spurred dynamic growth of the finance, banking, steel, timber, and myriad other industries. Unprecedented corporate power and business consolidation occurred, while (white European) immigrants flooded into the country and its burgeoning cities and towns in search of work and a better life.

The critical factor in the globalization of American imperialism was the evolution of a modern navy. In the early nineteenth century the Tripolitan War and the humiliation of the *Chesapeake* in 1807 had shown the vulnerability of the US Navy. Following the War of 1812, the Market Revolution brought increased foreign trade, advances in shipping and sailing and the transformation wrought by steam power. The emergence of major fishing, sealing, and whaling industries heightened the value of enhanced knowledge of the maritime world as well as the desire for a modern navy to protect coastlines and reinforce merchant shipping.

In 1841 the United States floated the first screw-propeller-powered warship, the USS *Princeton*. On Feb. 28, 1844, one of its cannons exploded during a demonstration firing on the Potomac, killing the secretary of state and the secretary of the navy who were presiding over the unveiling. The following year the nation opened the Naval Observatory in Washington, DC. By 1854 the United States had developed a small fleet of 18 steam-powered naval vessels, which still lagged well behind the 68 French and 141 British steamships.

The British "mother" country offered a clear example of the linkage between naval development and imperial power. The legendary exploits of Captain James Cook in three separate Pacific voyages from 1768-1779, before his death in a clash with Hawaiian islanders, had long inspired American sea power enthusiasts.

Cook's voyages were the model in 1838 as Congress authorized the United States Exploring Expedition of the South Atlantic and Pacific. Setting off with four ships but returning with only one as a result of storms, wear and tear, the expedition led by Navy Lieutenant Charles Wilkes traversed 85,000 miles and some 280 islands, charting and mapping reefs, shoals and coastlines and exploring Antarctica. The expedition produced multiple volumes of in-depth studies of plant and animal life as well as geography and geology of a vast maritime world.

Like Cook, Wilkes and his men clashed with Pacific islanders. Following the death of two of his men, including his nephew, Wilkes directed the massacre of some 87 Fiji islanders in 1840. A harsh military disciplinarian, Wilkes faced court martial upon his return to the United States and was convicted of inflicting illegal punishments on sailors. The accomplishments of the expedition overshadowed Wilkes's ruthlessness, however, hence he received a slap on the wrist and was accounted a national hero. For many years following the expedition, whalers, sealers, merchant ships and the US Navy drew on the knowledge the expedition had amassed.

After the Mexican War, the Oregon Treaty and the Gold Rush, Americans were poised to expand from the West coast across the Pacific. By the time of the Wilkes expedition the United States had gotten out ahead of imperial competitors for control of the Hawaiian Islands, which would anchor US expansion across the Pacific. Following Cook's first voyage to the Islands in 1778, Westerners began to intrude and incur resentment, which eventually led to Cook's death in a clash with defenders of the Hawaiian monarch in 1779.

Missionary Christianity was an underlying component of American imperialism across the Pacific, as it was in the era of "manifest destiny." In the 1820s American missionaries, mostly from New England, migrated to Hawaii to convert the natives to Christianity. Beginning in 1829 the United States, among other Western nations, sent warships to demand debt collection and property rights. Weakened like the North American Indians by exposure to European diseases, the native Hawaiians and their well-established monarchy could not fend off US commercial interests, which followed in the wake of the missionaries.

American capitalists subverted Hawaiian sovereignty by converting the land from communal into private property. In the last half of the nineteenth century the Americans steadily pushed the monarchy aside, took control of the islands by importing Asian labor and established immensely profitable sugar and pineapple plantations.

US imperialism thus took control of Hawaii through economic and cultural subversion rather than war. The threat of violence, however, hung over the "Bayonet Constitution," which was forced on the Hawaiians, stripping the kingdom of its authority in 1887. In 1893 the American occupiers overthrew the Hawaiian monarchy and absurdly proclaimed the existence of a new "republic." Five years later, amid the ebullience of the Spanish-American War, the United States abandoned all pretext and annexed Hawaii by joint resolution of the Congress.

The takeover of Hawaii provided the Navy with a Pacific outpost enhanced by the welcoming waters of Pearl Harbor. In 1867, the United States had annexed Midway Island, roughly halfway between North America and the Asian mainland. The United States now possessed important coaling stations to steam across the Pacific and compete with other Western imperial powers in Asia.

Another pillar of American trans-Pacific imperialism came with the purchase of Alaska from Russia in 1867. Once again--in a process that began with the American Revolution and received powerful momentum in the Louisiana Purchase--the United States claimed sovereignty over masses of indigenous people simply by signing a treaty with another European nation.

As in Hawaii and in contrast with North America, the United States gradually established authority in Alaska without resort to war. On at least a couple of occasions the US Army engaged in collective punishment, destroying entire villages in response to alleged assaults by indigenous Alaskans on white settlers. On another occasion the Army jailed an American in Sitka as a result of his having killed two native men, but quickly released him when the settlers protested. Thus, as historian Stephen Haycox notes, "The army and navy limited their activity to enforcing American justice, essentially without regard to Indian culture, Indian experience, or Indian dignity." The discovery of gold in the Klondike region sent settlers streaking to Canada's Yukon territory as well as Alaska, thus fueling settlement of the future forty-ninth state.

American imperialism in the Asia-Pacific region thus pivoted on the colonization of the future states of Alaska and Hawaii. In the 1840s the United States had begun to compete with the other Western imperial powers for treaty ports, trade, and influence in China, from which they imported labor to help mine precious metals and build the Western railroads. However, the United States as a latecomer could not match the footholds that Britain and France had already secured in East Asia.

Concerned that Great Britain would seek to monopolize trade with Japan, which futilely attempted to resist the intrusion of all Western "barbarians," the United States played a prominent role in "opening" Japan. In 1853 the Navy dispatched Commodore Matthew Perry with four ships, authorizing him to use intimidation and force if deemed necessary. Reaching Edo (Tokyo) Bay in July 1853, Perry ignored orders to leave, fired blank shots from his 73 cannons and demanded an audience with high-ranking Japanese officials. Allowed to make a landing after several days in the harbor, Perry did so with pomp and ceremony, firing his guns and striking up the band to play "Hail Columbia." He presented a letter from President Millard Fillmore demanding the opening of trade with the United States before departing with a promise that he would return in expectation of receiving an official reply.

Aware that the Russians as well as the French and British were stepping up their own demands on Japan, Perry returned in 1854 with a formidable armada of 10 ships. The Shogunate, which had decided to meet most of Fillmore's demands, authorized a landing at Yokohama. Perry marched ashore with 500 sailors while the band played the "Star Spangled Banner."

During the ensuing negotiations Perry emphasized that the United States had defeated Mexico in war and "circumstances may lead your country into a similar plight" should Japan fail to negotiate a satisfactory accord. In March the Japanese signed off on the Treaty of Kanagawa opening two treaty ports to the Americans, granted most favored nation trade status, provisions for repatriating shipwrecked sailors, and the opening of a US consulate. Perry followed up by forging a treaty with the Ryukyu Kingdom, which he had also provocatively "opened" through the same style of gunboat diplomacy. The following year Perry returned home a hero, was awarded $20,000 (about $600,000 in 2021 dollars) and promoted to rear admiral.

Japan naturally resented the foreign intrusions and in 1863 attacked American, French, British, and Dutch targets, including burning the US legation in Tokyo. Embroiled in the Civil War, the United States let the other countries take the lead, but did dispatch the USS *Wyoming*, which sank two Japanese vessels while suffering 14 casualties in the fight. The other nations subdued the Japanese, who vowed never again to be dominated by foreigners and embarked on the Meiji Restoration to modernize and gain strength.

In 1866, as it strove to open the "hermit kingdom" of Korea, the United States sent the armed and aptly named merchant ship the *General Sherman* upriver to Pyongyang, where it entered into a bloody clash with the resistant Koreans. The American ship fired into crowds but the Koreans fought back with fireboats, killing a couple of crewmen.

In 1871 a US force of 600 men invaded with attack boats backed by two battleships from the Asiatic Squadron in what became the largest military engagement involving American forces between the Civil War and the War with Spain in 1898. Three Americans died while killing more than 240 Koreans in the massacre, which the *New York Herald* called the "Little War with the Heathen." In 1882 the United States secured a treaty with Korea for most favored nation trade status and extraterritoriality.

In 1889 the United States competed aggressively with Britain and Germany over control of Samoa, a grouping of 14 islands along the South Pacific trade routes to Australia and New Zealand. The Americans took the conflict to the edge of war at which point a massive hurricane damaged the Western holdings in the islands and created a climate conducive to a diplomatic settlement. The three imperialist powers partitioned the islands, but the United States received the top prize, the favorable harbor at Pago Pago, giving the Americans the inside track facilitating eventual annexation of the islands.

By this time the US drive for Asian-Pacific imperialism had broad support among some commercial interests, Protestant missionaries, sea power enthusiasts, and proponents of the rise of the United States to world power. At the US Naval War College, created in 1885, Alfred Thayer Mahan lectured on the relationship between sea power and global influence throughout history. In 1890 Mahan, who came from a military family, published his lectures in book form as *The Influence of Sea Power Upon History*, 1660-1782, which quickly became the preeminent work on the subject, published in myriad languages and circulated worldwide.

Mahan emphasized that if the United States was to transition from a mere continental nation into a world power, it must cultivate a powerful navy, including a fleet of state-of-the-art battleships, facilitated by overseas bases. There was nothing especially original about the central argument but Mahan made it well and it caught the attention of important people, including the influential Senator Henry Cabot Lodge (R-MA) and the rising political star from New York, Theodore Roosevelt.

Mahan, Lodge, Roosevelt, and other imperialists championed a buildup of American naval power and longed for the nation to take its "rightful" place as a world power. They not only would not shy away from war they relished the opportunities for individual and national glory that war might bring. The decaying Spanish Empire offered an ideal target for a campaign of imperial aggression that would vault the United States into the ranks of the leading world powers.

The "Spanish-American" War

The so-called Spanish-American War involved fighting in neither Spain nor North America, rather it was fought out in the Caribbean and in Southeast Asia. As with most wars in American history, the United States chose to go to war despite facing no threat to its own security. The Spanish-American War was at its essence an offensive war for empire. Spanish maladministration of Cuba created an opportunity to go to war. Spain was an "Old World" empire in decline whereas the United States was a rising empire that had announced decades previously—in the 1823 Monroe Doctrine—that it intended to supervise the Western Hemisphere.

American imperialism in Cuba had a protracted history. "Founding fathers" including Thomas Jefferson and John Quincy Adams believed that Cuba, as Adams once put it, inevitably would "gravitate" toward the United States. In the antebellum era a filibusterer named Narciso Lopez, backed by US business interests and American mercenaries, tried to foment a coup in Cuba, but he was captured and executed by the Spanish in Havana in 1851. Three years later proslavery Southern diplomats, meeting secretly in Belgium, plotted in what became known as the Ostend Manifesto to "detach" Cuba from Spain and turn it into a thriving slave state. Had not the Civil War intervened, a war with Spain and attempts to bring Cuba into the Union might have occurred earlier. The United States remained keen on Caribbean expansion after the Civil War, as Secretary of State William Seward tried to purchase Santo Domingo, but Congress rejected the initiative as a result of lingering sectional divisions as well as the foul odor of Grant-era political scandals.

The Cubans, meanwhile, demanded their own liberation and from 1868-78 fought a rebellion that Spain managed to repress. By the 1890s, with the Cubans again mounting resistance, Spain instituted a brutal re-concentration program killing and imprisoning alleged rebels. The American press publicized the conflict to an increasingly literate American public that became enamored with the idea of "liberating" Cuba from its Monroe Doctrine-violating, Catholic European oppressor.

President William McKinley, who had been a Union officer in the Civil War, dispatched the battleship *Maine* to make a provocative appearance in Havana Harbor. On Feb. 15, 1898, 250 US sailors and marines died as the *Maine* suddenly exploded. Americans widely assumed Spain had planted a bomb on the ship, but it may be, as subsequent studies concluded, that the ship's volatile coal bins ignited in a spontaneous explosion. In any case, the destruction of the *Maine* increased pressure on McKinley--whose "backbone" was called into question by critics and the penny press—to go to war.

Roosevelt and others openly advocated an aggressive war through which the United States would achieve a "higher manhood" and take its place at the pinnacle of world power. McKinley gave in to the pressure, abandoning diplomacy even as Spain had begun to back down, and asked Congress for a declaration of war, which the House provided overwhelmingly but the Senate only narrowly by a vote of 42-35. The Senate might not have approved at all but for an amendment sponsored by Colorado Senator Henry Teller renouncing any US plan to annex Cuba.

As national patriotism skyrocketed, more than a million volunteers streamed into enlistment centers, but the enthusiasm masked a striking level of unpreparedness and disorganization reminiscent of the War of 1812. Roosevelt, who emerged from the war a hero, begged in the midst of the conflict for the provision of food and basic necessities for the troops. He declared the war effort was on "the very verge of disaster," as "the mismanagement has been beyond belief." In 1969 two government historians, one an Army officer, judged the war effort "incompetent" and "unbecoming a nation on the eve of becoming a world power."

Fortunately for the United States, Spain was even less well organized, lacked an emotional commitment to the fight, and had to contend with freedom-seeking Cubans as well as the American invaders. The Cubans played a key role in providing the Americans with intelligence while stepping up their own guerrilla resistance. The United States gave the Cubans no credit for the subsequent victory, prevented them from taking part in the Spanish surrender, and would soon prevent Cuba from fulfilling its aspirations of becoming a free and independent republic.

Actual fighting centered around an attack on Santiago from which the Spanish ultimately retreated. While General Nelson Miles, the "hero" of Wounded Knee, attacked the Spanish in Santiago the US Navy seized Guantanamo and from there hemmed in the Spanish fleet in Santiago Bay on Cuba's southeast coast. After a highly disorganized embarkation from Tampa, Roosevelt's and other volunteer forces arrived to take part in the famous charge up San Juan Hill. The attacking force of regular army troops, Roosevelt's Rough Riders, and segregated forces of African-American "Buffalo soldiers" took the hill, but suffered 205 dead and 1,180 wounded. The Spanish fleet made a break for it out of the harbor, enabling the Navy to sink two of the ships and cripple others, killing some 300 Spanish sailors to one American death in the massacre at sea.

Bolstered by thousands of reinforcements after being decimated by tropical disease and poor provisions, the army sailed from Guantanamo Bay to Puerto Rico. Miles encountered little resistance as Puerto Rico quickly fell to the Americans. Spain capitulated and the "splendid little war" was over in a matter of weeks. The United States suffered 385 killed in battle, about half of Spain's body count, but more than 2,000 Americans and 15,000 Spaniards died of disease. Poor provisions and lack of medical supplies led many soldiers to die in agony.

Unable to annex Cuba because of the Teller amendment in the US Senate, the United States settled for a more subtle form of imperialism, a protectorate in which it reserved the right to intervene militarily, a "right" that it would exercise on several occasions to maintain control over the island's economy and politics. Americans, in short, did not liberate Cuba or Puerto Rico. The latter remains an American colony to this day.

American Imperialism and War

Taking the Philippines

Much to the surprise of most Americans, the first front of the Spanish-American War was in Southeast Asia. In contrast to Cuba, so little publicity had been focused on the Philippines that few Americans even knew that the islands were a Spanish colony, much less where they were located. But the naval power imperialists knew exactly where the archipelago was and it was Roosevelt, serving at the time as assistant secretary of the navy, who had put the Navy in position to attack Spain across the Pacific.

On May 1, 1898, Admiral George Dewey crushed the decrepit Spanish fleet in a naval massacre in Manila Harbor. In short order Spain lost seven ships and 350 men compared with one American sailor who died from heat exhaustion. News of the lopsided victory prompted 100,000 people to pour into New York's Madison Square for a spontaneous celebration, a giddy excitement over imperial conquest that reverberated across the country.

The Filipinos, who like the Cubans shared a developing national consciousness and had long struggled for independence from Spain, greeted Dewey warmly when he arrived on shore. Dewey assured them that the United States was a republic and did not intend to colonize the islands. That decision was not his, however, and the naval enthusiasts backed by much of the public prevailed upon McKinley, who decided the United States would assume authority over the "little brown brothers" in order to "uplift and civilize them and Christianize them." Most of the Philippines, however, had already long been Christianized by Spain. McKinley was actually most keen about the "commercial opportunities to which American statesmanship cannot be indifferent."

Exercising its well-established prerogative of purchasing other lands and people, the United States paid Spain $20 million for the Philippines, which it now annexed along with Hawaii, Samoa, and Guam--which also had been colonized by the Spanish—and Wake Island as well. Named for a Briton, Wake Island had been surveyed by Wilkes in 1841 but now formally became an outpost of the growing American empire on the Pacific.

The Filipinos, whose charismatic national leader, Jose Rizal, had been martyred by the Spanish in 1896, were now led by Emilio Aguinaldo, who had spearheaded the resistance against Spain. As with the Cubans, the Americans showed racist disdain for Aguinaldo, labeled "a Chinese half-breed," as they hoisted the Stars and Stripes in Manila. The press and public officials referred to the multi-ethnic Philippines as an inchoate amalgamation of "tribes" which like the North American Indians were

63

unable to govern themselves and would have to be shepherded toward civilization.

Aguinaldo and his followers had no intention of bowing to the replacement of one Western interloper by another. In order to pacify the islands, the United States would thus have to wage a bloody counterinsurgency war. The Americans would call it the Philippine "Insurrection," as if it were an uprising against legitimate authority. In actuality it was a Filipino struggle for national liberation from a long legacy of European and now American imperialism.

Street battles erupted in and around Manila in the first week of February 1899 and from there spread into the countryside. The US press and public, overwhelmingly enthusiastic about war and imperialism, were shocked and angered by the Filipino resistance. No less an authority than the *New York Times* declared that the Filipinos' "insane attack . . . on their liberators" was alone proof of "their incapacity for self-government."

As the Philippine rebels engaged in sabotage, sniping, and stabbing attacks with their *bolos* (long knives), the Americans condemned the resort to guerrilla war as atavistic and dishonorable. Citing the "barbarous savagery" of the Philippine resistance, the United States embarked on a campaign of indiscriminate warfare replete with assassination, massacres, confinement, collective punishment, and torture.

Declaring that "every Filipino was really an insurgent," General Elwell Otis, the American military governor, authorized lethal patrols in the cities and into the "boondocks" (from the Tagalog term for mountains). US forces embarked on explicitly racist search-and-destroy indiscriminate killing missions across the archipelago. A soldier from Kansas neatly linked the racialized killing with the home front, explaining that the islands would not be pacified "until the niggers are killed off like the Indians." As in previous American wars, volunteers and some regulars episodically engaged in indiscriminate attacks as well as looting and sexual assault.

After a widely publicized surprise attack in which 48 US soldiers were killed on a Sunday morning at Balangiga in Samar province in September 1901, US commanders authorized a genocidal response to the "treacherous savagery" of the native. "I want no prisoners," General Jacob Smith—another "hero" of Wounded Knee--advised. Vowing to turn Samar into a biblical "howling wilderness," he commanded troops to "kill and burn. The more you kill and burn the better you will please me." The Army subsequently brought Smith before a court-martial in which he was convicted for violating the laws of war, but he was merely admonished and forced to retire. Killing natives thus continued to go unpunished in American history.

The massive death toll of at least 250,000 and possibly as many as 800,000 Filipinos stemmed overwhelmingly from famine and disease rather than direct killing. US patrols destroyed farms and villages as they carried out what historians have described as "ecological destruction on a massive scale," producing an "astoundingly high level of civilian mortality." The Americans crammed suspected guerrillas into internment camps, where disease spread rapidly. Suspected guerrillas were subjected to torture including widespread use of simulated drowning in the "water cure." More than a century later the practice would be resurrected and referenced as "waterboarding" amid the US invasion and occupation of Iraq.

Winning Hearts and Minds

While the "Philippine insurrection" was beyond question an atrocity-filled "dirty war," it was at the same time arguably one of the most successful counterinsurgency campaigns in US history. Even as they were killing outright or causing the deaths of masses of Filipinos, the United States at the same time engaged in an ambitious program of internal improvements designed to win the proverbial "hearts and minds" of the populace.

McKinley had promised a campaign of "benevolent assimilation" in which the United State would "win the confidence, respect and affection of the inhabitants." The Army as well as educators and health professionals made concerted efforts to achieve that goal. The United States orchestrated visible improvements in health, education, and infrastructure development that helped to legitimate the occupation in the eyes of some Filipino elites.

Improving Philippine society was not merely an end in itself but rather part of a broader campaign of war and colonization. The US Army built roads, bridges, sewers and sanitation facilities, hospitals, and schoolhouses to facilitate the colonial occupation. Americans set up literacy programs, invested significant efforts in disease control, and carried out municipal, legal, economic, educational, and judicial reforms. Some Filipinos cooperated enthusiastically with the civic action aspect of pacification even as they continued to resist military subjugation.

As in the Indian wars, the Americans also recruited informants, scouts and created auxiliary forces to assist with pacification efforts. The Philippines, which had not functioned to this point as a united nation, was fractured along myriad ethnic, social, regional, economic, and religious lines that US imperialism could exploit, thus creating a situation in which the people fought not only against the Americans but also against each other.

The combination of forces—mass killing, disease, famine, internal improvements, and divisions and disorganization among Filipinos—eventually enabled the United States to quell the guerrilla resistance. The occupation forces shrewdly coopted Filipino elites with incentives while stepping up propaganda and psychological warfare efforts against the insurgency. The capture of Aguinaldo in March 1901 deprived the rebel movement of its leader and prompted other insurgents to surrender to the Americans.

On July 4, 1902, concluding with an Orwellian flourish, the United States declared the "insurrection" defeated and the Philippines "liberated." Despite this claim, resistance and repression continued for another decade in predominately Muslim Mindanao, the second largest island located in the far south of the archipelago. A toxic combination of religious prejudice, racism, and indiscriminate warfare fueled the brutal repression replete with massacres in "Moro-land," as the Americans dubbed the Muslim south. The United States initially established a modus vivendi with the leaders in Mindanao, but after defeating the rebels to the north the sultanate rejected being governed by the Catholic-dominated Filipino elite.

General Leonard Wood, a Roosevelt confidante and fellow Rough Rider hero, carried out the campaign against the "religious and moral degenerates" in the south, whose leader, he decided, was of "the Geronimo type." In March 1906 Wood unleashed repeated artillery barrages killing at least 600 "Moro malcontents," including unarmed women and children. In 1913 the Army was still trying to rein in "the most aggressive and determined Orientals," as it unleashed what one scholar described as an "asymmetric bloodbath" slaughtering between 300 and 400 people compared to 14 US deaths at Bud Bagsak. The brutal pacification program carried out by the Army and Filipino allies finally ended the following year.

By the time the United States turned over pacification to Filipino elites, the islands had been transformed. Rather than being established as a viable republic, the archipelago would be governed by a minority elite, backed by a ubiquitous secret-police, and susceptible to strong-man rule, as a result of an absence of checks and balances on executive authority. An oligarchy of business elites, local bosses, and interconnected political families stifled reform and enabled corruption within the security state that was first erected by the American occupation and subsequently propelled by Filipino elites with continuing US assistance.

The Filipino regime enabled continuing US military occupation establishing the Philippines as a key outpost, punctuating the rise of the United States as a Pacific and world power. The new Pacific empire was anchored by a sprawling new naval base at Subic Bay and in later years an airbase, Clark Field. Underscoring the significance of the Philippines, these became for a time the two largest US overseas military bases in the world.

Profoundly consequential, American imperialism and war across the Pacific culminating in the Philippines set the stage for future interventions in China, Japan, Korea, and Vietnam, among others. The first but not the last counterinsurgency war fought by the United States in Southeast Asia, the Philippine conflict resulted in the deaths of more than 4,200 US soldiers and the wounding of some 2,800, a small percentage of the massive toll the asymmetrical war exacted on the Philippines. The fact that hundreds of thousands of Filipinos were killed as a result of American imperialism is rarely acknowledged and little appreciated. For all of the reasons discussed, the Philippine war was one of the most significant yet also one of the most often overlooked or marginalized overseas conflicts in American history.

While violently subduing the Filipinos, Americans condemned European imperialism in China, but only because they wanted a piece of the action. In 1899 and 1900 the United States sent the "Open Door Notes" condemning exclusive spheres of influence in China. However, in 1900 US Marines joined the European interlopers in subduing the anti-imperialist Boxer Rebellion in Beijing.

By the turn of the century the United States had cultivated a fleet of battleships named for individual states and had begun to catch up with the navies of Britain, Germany, and China. In 1907 Roosevelt, who rose to the presidency with the assassination of McKinley in September 1901, dispatched the appropriately named Great White Fleet—16 battleships in four squadrons, all painted a gleaming white—in a show of force across the Pacific. In October 1908, in sharp contrast with Perry's visit a half-century earlier, the fleet received a cordial welcome in Tokyo Bay. Japan's defeat of Russia in war in 1905 had earned the respect of Roosevelt and others. In 1908 the United States and Japan signed an accord recognizing each other's spheres of influence in East Asia.

Professionalization of the Army accompanied the turn of the century burst of US imperialism. In 1903 the Army War College opened its doors with the purpose of educating senior officers in the wake of the woeful disorganization and command structure that prevailed at the start of the war with Spain. Drawing on a deeply-rooted American tradition of state-centered militias, the 1903 Militia Act created the National Guard of Organized Militia and Reserve Militia. The National Guard, as it became known, began to conduct training exercises and maneuvers with regular Army units.

Anti-Imperialism and Cultural Hegemony

The blatant US imperialism in the Caribbean as well as Southeast Asia precipitated one of the more spirited anti-imperialist movements in the nation's history. Domestic opposition to American wars was nothing new, though none had succeeded in impeding imperialism and war. At least half the population had been loyal to Britain in the Revolutionary War; most Federalists opposed the War of 1812; a vocal minority decried "Mr. Polk's war" with Mexico; and Eastern humanitarians had condemned the brutal subjugation of Indians. The imperial thrusts beyond the continent beginning in 1898 and carrying into the Philippines forged the first truly national antiwar movement, albeit one centered like previous such efforts in New England and along the East Coast.

In November 1898, six months after Admiral Dewey's glorious triumph in Manila Bay, the Anti-Imperialist League, chartered in Boston, declared opposition to the extension of US sovereignty over "foreign territory, without the free consent of the people thereof," in violation of "constitutional principles, and fraught with moral and physical evils to our people." Many luminaries, including former President Grover Cleveland, diplomat Charles Francis Adams, philanthropist Andrew Carnegie, Stanford President David Starr Jordan, settlement house pioneer Jane Addams, and labor leader Samuel Gompers helped mobilize a nationwide movement.

For most Americans the martial triumph and arrival on the stage as a world power eclipsed concerns about immoral usurpation of the rights to self-government of other peoples, who were, after all, it was widely believed, racially inferior and uncivilized. In fact, many anti-imperialists such as the liberal editor of *The Nation*, E.L. Godkin, argued against imperialism on the basis that it would undermine America's racial purity through the incorporation of "alien, inferior, mongrel races."

Campaigning in his Rough Rider uniform as McKinley's vice-presidential nominee in 1900, Roosevelt led the charge against the anti-imperialists as he rejected their suggestion that the subjugation and domination of foreign people was somehow un-American. The United States was making "no new departure," Roosevelt declared, noting the conflicts were "precisely parallel between the Philippines and the Apaches and the Sioux." Reports of US atrocities in the islands were nothing new either, Roosevelt explained, noting that they "happened hundreds of times in our warfare against the Indians" and were inevitable byproducts of the march of civilization over savagery. In a similar vein Senator Lodge tellingly declared that if subjugation of the Philippines was a crime, as anti-imperialist charged, "then our whole past record of expansion is a crime."

McKinley's decisive reelection victory over anti-imperialist William Jennings Bryan largely resolved the issue as another defeat for anti-imperialism in American history.

From 1876 to 1916 a series of international exhibitions attended by millions of Americans offered reassurance that what was unfolding was merely the inevitable triumph of civilization over savagery. As Americans fortified segregation at home and imperialism abroad, displays such as the World Columbian Exhibition, held at Chicago's White City in 1893, emphasized white supremacy and Social Darwinism. William "Buffalo Bill" Cody's long-running Wild West shows delighted audiences with its glorification of subduing the wild Indians. In 1901 the Pan-American Exposition at Buffalo pursued an explicit directive "to justify . . . the acquisition of new territory." The same exhibition also featured the "Darkest Africa," "Old Plantation," and "The American Negro" displays reinforcing the backwardness of blackness and thereby affirming white supremacy. In the Louisiana Purchase Exhibition in St. Louis in 1904, as well as subsequent displays, Filipinos were brought in and dressed in loin cloths to lend authenticity to representation of "barbaric tribes" being provided the blessings of civilization by a superior people.

Establishing Caribbean Hegemony

As the US public internalized imperialism, the United States solidified its control over Cuba. The Teller amendment had precluded annexation in 1898 but in 1901 Secretary of War Elihu Root, a corporate attorney, established a legal framework for continuing US hegemony over the island. The Platt Amendment, drafted by Root but formally introduced by Senator Orville Platt (R-CT), explicitly sanctioned the US "right to intervene" militarily, which it exercised by sending in troops to assert authority from 1906-09, again in 1912 and in 1917.

The US Navy expanded the base at Guantanamo Bay, which it secured in perpetuity through an unequal treaty with the US-dominated Cuban government in 1903. The base anchored the emerging US naval domination of the Caribbean Sea. Investors from the mainland flooded in to take control of the profitable Cuban sugar and railroad industries. As it had done in the Philippines, the United Sates coopted Cuban elites, precluding broader social welfare initiatives, and carried out internal improvements, including sanitation and health reforms that helped to eradicate yellow fever.

More compact and modernized than Cuba, Puerto Rico, designated an "unincorporated territory" by the Foraker Act (1900), became an American colony. The United States established a coaling station on the island for the Navy and, as in Cuba, carried out internal improvements while orienting the sugar industry toward the American export market.

Roosevelt presided over the US Caribbean hegemony, which he reinforced through unilateral construction, control, and military occupation of the Panama Canal Zone. In 1903, after Colombia rejected the terms of a treaty giving the United States exclusive rights to dig a canal in its province of Panama, Roosevelt fomented a coup backed by a gunboat, the USS *Nashville*, which along with some timely payoffs in gold succeeded in detaching Panama from Colombia. Washington then signed a canal treaty with a French builder (the treaty "that no Panamanian ever signed," as it became known). Although he lied about fomenting the coup at the time, the Rough Rider president later admitted, "I took Panama and let Congress debate."

The coup in Panama, like the coup in Hawaii that ushered in the Bayonet Constitution, established precedents that would become a regular pattern of behavior carried out by the "top secret" Central Intelligence Agency in the post-World War II era.

After detaching Panama, Roosevelt subsequently pronounced his Corollary to the Monroe Doctrine. He advised the Europeans to refrain from intervention in the region for the purpose of debt collection, which the United States pledged to do for them, along with taking any other actions that might be needed to advance the cause of "civilization" throughout the Americas.

Roosevelt's successor, William Howard Taft, a corporate attorney and former governor-general of the occupied Philippines, orchestrated US economic domination of the islands as well as the nations of Central America. "Dollar diplomacy," as the policy was known, was intended to avoid direct military intervention, which a minority of anti-imperialists condemned. However, as events unfolded the United States continued to engage in "gunboat diplomacy" and landing of marines in the region.

From 1898 to 1920 US forces landed at least 20 times to reinforce imperialism in Central America and the Caribbean. In addition to the "protectorates" over Cuba and Puerto Rico and domination of the Panama Canal Zone, the United States launched a major intervention to quell unrest in Nicaragua, sending the Marines on aggressive patrols against rebels in the countryside. Nicaraguans had been hostile to Yankee intervention for decades, recalling that during the antebellum era the American filibusterer William Walker had invaded the country, proclaimed himself its president in 1856, and legalized slavery. Walker was eventually driven into the sea (and later executed in Honduras) but not before his forces killed hundreds if not thousands of Nicaraguans, raped women, and torched the historic city of Granada.

The US marines occupied Nicaragua from 1912 to 1925 and again from 1927 to 1933, at which point the United States ensconced the family dictatorship of Anastasio Somoza, which went on to plunder the country for decades. Washington sent troops into neighboring Honduras from 1912 to 1919 and again in 1924-25, transforming the Central American nation into the quintessential "banana republic." In addition to control of banana exports by the United Fruit Company, US mining, railroad, shipping and banking industries dominated the Central American economies, whose residents, other than a minority of elites and state police forces, remained impoverished.

The United States also militarily occupied Haiti (1915-1934) and the Dominican Republic (1916-1924). Rejecting the concept of a "black republic," the United States had opposed the Haitian revolution against France at the turn of the nineteenth century. More than century later, President Woodrow Wilson explained that the "misbehavior" of the residents of Haiti, which he called "the dusky little republic," necessitated the Marine invasion of 1915. Thousands of Haitians were killed during the ensuing 20-year occupation. Some Marines related the violent policing of Haitians to the ongoing pattern of lynching, subjugation and popular depiction of African Americans on the home front.

Peace activists and progressive internationalists criticized the Caribbean military occupations, pointing out that such interventions failed to promote democracy. By 1933 liberal criticism prompted the newly inaugurated President Franklin D. Roosevelt to announce a new "Good Neighbor Policy." Roosevelt renounced direct US military intervention in the region and brought an end to the long-running Nicaraguan and Haitian occupations.

Invading Mexico, Again

While the Caribbean occupations brought episodic violent repression, the American intervention in Mexico nearly produced a full-scale war. Popular resentment had been building in Mexico over US economic penetration of the country under the dictatorship of Porfirio Diaz, who had ruled since 1876 and thrown Mexico open to Yankee economic domination. The United States controlled 75 percent of Mexico's mines and half of its oil fields while some 50,000 Americans resided in Mexico.

In 1906 a strike by workers in northern Sonora prompted the US owners of the mines to summon across the border a posse of Arizona rangers, killing more than 20 of the workers. Over the next few years Mexico's rural and urban poor mounted increasing protests, finally toppling the decrepit Diaz regime in 1911. As the Mexican Revolution unleashed widespread political instability, scores of Americans living in Mexico lost their lives and property.

Amid this tumult an otherwise innocuous incident at Tampico was escalated into a direct US military intervention. On April 9, 1914, a US Navy whaleboat was refueling at the Atlantic coastal city when a Mexican patrol arrested and jailed the small crew. They were immediately released by higher authorities at which point Admiral Henry T. Mayo, commander of the Navy squadron, demanded not only a written apology but also that the Mexican army "hoist the American flag on a prominent position on shore and salute it with twenty-one guns."

Mexico naturally refused to be subjected to the humiliating exercise. President Wilson responded by landing several hundred US Marines at Mexico's principal port of Vera Cruz. Once again, after a 70-year hiatus, the Yankees were invading Mexico.

At Vera Cruz the Americans sought to intercept an arms shipment from Germany intended for Mexican General Victoriana Huerta, who had ordered the assassination of Mexico's elected president Francisco Madero. In a clash with Mexican forces, 80 Americans died while the Mexicans suffered some 300 casualties. Wilson subsequently accepted mediation from Argentina, Brazil and Chile but that did not bring an end to the conflict with Mexico.

On March 9, 1916, Mexican rebel leader Francisco "Pancho" Villa, angry over Wilson's support of the new Mexican Constitutionalist government, conducted a cross-border raid against US Army forces barracked in the town of Columbus, New Mexico. Villa's forces killed 25 Americans, 10 of them soldiers, but suffered some 100 dead on its own as a result of the alert Army response, which quickly forced Villa to retreat back across the border.

Villa's attack outraged Wilson, who authorized General John "Black Jack" Pershing, a veteran of the Indian and Philippine wars, to mount an expedition deep into Mexico in an effort to capture Villa. By April 8 Pershing and an army of 6,675 men had penetrated 400 miles into Mexican territory, skirmished with Mexican armed forces, causing a few dozen casualties on both sides, and incurring the wrath of the Mexican people, who provided little help in locating Villa. During the feckless intervention the United States conducted its largest-ever mobilization of the relatively new National Guard, dispatched to protect the border, and for the first time, used trucks to transport supplies and airplanes to conduct aerial reconnaissance, all in a vain effort to locate Villa and his band.

In February 1917, following an 11-month intervention, the United States withdrew its forces. By that time, a much larger and more consequential war had erupted in Europe and was spreading across the globe.

Chapter 5
Entering in a World of Wars

The two world wars in the first half of the twentieth century utterly transformed American foreign policy and the nation's place in the world. Fueled by the cultural hegemony of American exceptionalism—the protean "mission" to make the world "safe for democracy"--intervention in World War I proved to be a disaster both at home and abroad. In the Second World War, Americans celebrated victory, but the conflict had sweeping unforeseen consequences, including the permanent militarization of American foreign policy spawning a series of future imperial wars.

In George Washington's Farewell Address (1796) as well as the Monroe Doctrine (1823), the United States had established as a cardinal tenet of US foreign policy the avoidance of direct involvement in European power politics. The nation adhered to that approach until the "great departure" of April 1917.

The outbreak of the Great War in August 1914 initially elicited a firm declaration of neutrality from President Wilson. As the conflict unfolded, however, a majority of Americans sympathized with the Triple Entente (Britain, France and Russia) over the Central Powers (Germany, Austria-Hungary, and the Ottoman Empire), particularly in the wake of the shocking sinking by a German U-Boat (submarine) in May 1915 of the British luxury liner, the *Lusitania*, in which 128 Americans were among the 1,201 dead.

Wilson famously campaigned and won reelection in 1916 behind the slogan, "He kept us out of the war," but the president's commitment to neutrality eroded over Germany's renewal of unrestricted submarine warfare and the threat that "the Huns" might win the war and dominate Europe politically and economically. The United States had far more trade and cultural ties with the Entente powers, especially Britain, and US banks had loaned money to them, which they might not be able to redeem in the event of victory by the Central Powers.

In February, British intelligence supplied the United States with the intercepted Zimmermann Telegram in which the German foreign minister had invited Mexico to join in war in order to get back some of the territory lost to the Americans in the past century. The offer naturally increased US public antipathy toward Germany even though Mexico was in no position to seriously consider taking up the offer.

Coinciding with the publication of the Zimmermann Telegram, the collapse of the inept tsarist regime in Russia paved the way for Wilson to make the case that an allied victory would advance democracy, now that the autocratic regime had fallen to a parliamentary provisional government. No one could have known that the new liberal Russian government would be overthrown in October after only a few months in power.

By 1917 the Great War had become the most widespread and destructive conflict in world history. Massive battle fields, devastating trench warfare, poison gas attacks, and failed offensives marked by horrifying casualties characterized the conflict. In this context the deeply religious Wilson began to view the United States (and himself) as a potential savior. He decided to enter the war by framing it as a "war to end all wars," a grand crusade to make the world "safe for democracy." In the first week of April, Congress declared war on Germany by votes of 82-6 in the Senate and 373-50 in the House.

The United States thus chose to enter the European conflict and did so in a state of unpreparedness. The Army had gained experience in using motorized transport and deploying airplanes in Mexico, but as military historians note, "the US Army in 1917 was not a modern army." It lacked tanks, aircraft, artillery, and warfighting experience. The National Defense Act of 1916 had strengthened federal supervision over the National Guard. The Naval Act of the same year, designed primarily to counter Japan in the Pacific, emphasized development of capital ships and surface warfare but offered little to counter the threat of submarine warfare.

As in previous wars the United States also entered the Great War with a less than united public. Because as in most American wars World War I was a war of choice rather than necessity many people were opposed to it.

While most Americans sympathized with the allies, many Irish Americans, angered by British suppression of the Easter Rebellion (1916) in Ireland, and German Americans, among others, did not share the majority opinion. African Americans noted the hypocrisy of the United States--a country in which they lacked civil and voting rights and were still being lynched in the South--crusading to make the world "safe for democracy." Women, who still lacked national suffrage, noted the same contradiction. Socialists, prominent in the reform-oriented Progressive Era, condemned both sides for the "capitalist" and "imperialist" war.

None of this boded well for the future and indeed the United States would exit the war in the fall of 1918 far more divided than when it began.

Over There

Underscoring his fervent belief in American exceptionalism, Wilson emphasized that the United States entered the war not as an allied but rather as an "associated" power. As head of the American Expeditionary Force (AEF) he tapped "Black Jack" Pershing, the West Point graduate who had decades of military experience in campaigns against the Apache as well as the Muslims of Mindanao and most recently in his futile search for Pancho Villa in Mexico. In May 1917 Pershing arrived in France with a small staff and set about making plans to command the largest US army to be fielded since the Civil War.

The nation faced the challenge of mobilizing for a war in which the United States had not been attacked, which might otherwise fuel a deeper national commitment and spur a larger number of volunteers. In May 1917 Congress passed the Selective Service Act, which despite the deliberate choice of the benign term "service" was a compulsory draft, one that many Americans—as in the Civil War—opposed out of principle as well as self-preservation. Widespread evasion ("slackers") notwithstanding, the United States for the first time mobilized a truly national army, as more than 70 percent of the US forces in the Great War would be draftees.

While young men were loaded onto ships and dispatched to a foreign continent to be put in harm's way, bankers and industrialists were set up to profit from US intervention. The world war produced unprecedented collusion between the federal government and private banking and industry. The War Industries Board, headed by Wall Street financier Bernard Baruch, mobilized corporations behind the war effort by offering fixed prices and guaranteed profits. Government antitrust actions, all the rage earlier in the century, virtually ceased. Absent oversight and regulation, corruption was widespread. The banking, arms, shipbuilding, chemical and other war industries took off, spawning what in later years would become known as the "military-industrial complex."

On the ground in Europe fighting centered on the Western front, particularly when Russia, now led by the communist Bolsheviks following their takeover in October, withdrew from the war in a separate peace with Germany in March 1918. Germany made an all-out effort to win the war before the AEF could become mobilized and make an impact, but a major offensive failed.

After tremendous dislocations and bottlenecks in getting supplies to the American forces streaming into France, the AEF took up the fight. in May US forces helped to blunt the German offensive by taking the village of Cantigny. In September 1918 the Americans drove the Germans out of St. Mihiel, suffering 7,000 casualties in the process.

The much-celebrated triumph at St. Mihiel masked Pershing's flaws as a commander. Notoriously inflexible and determined to retain sole authority over the US war effort, Pershing quickly alienated his "associated" military partners. He then hurled American forces into battle in an aggressive "open war" strategy of attack. In so doing he failed to learn from the Europeans' woeful experiences of assaulting entrenched positions filled with machine-gun nests. He thus bears some responsibility for the high rate of American casualties, especially in the Meuse-Argonne Offensive that stretched across the entire Western front in the fall of 1918.

More than a million US troops--hastily trained "doughboys" with no previous experience in combat--took part in the massive offensive. The role of naval power was limited amid the grinding European conflict, but the Navy nonetheless grew more than ten-fold during the war, from 65,000 to more than 600,000 men in uniform. The Navy's primary role, securing supply convoys, was unglamorous but no less essential to the war effort as the United States carried out by far the largest overseas military supply operation in world history. The reorganized National Guard gained prominence, as it comprised nearly a fifth of the AEF.

American airpower, championed by Colonel and then General Billy Mitchell, launched a massive raid on German troop concentrations east of the Meuse River. At the same time the nation's top "ace," Eddie Rickenbacker, was ringing up victories in aerial dog fights, publicizing the rising role of airpower in modern warfare.

Exhausted by the war and increasingly divided on the home front, Germany sued for peace on the basis of Wilson's idealistic democratic framework, the Fourteen Points. On November 11, 1918, the signing of the armistice brought an end to the devastating conflict.

More than two million American men had served in France; more than 116,000 died. More than half of the deaths stemmed from accidents and disease, a figure that rose sharply as a consequence of the 1918 influenza pandemic. Some 204,000 Americans were wounded in the Great War. The US casualty figure was high for only a few months of direct fighting, but it was a mere fraction of what the European nations had suffered.

Even after the armistice some US forces remained embroiled in conflict in Russia, where the United States had intervened, partly to assist a legion of Czech troops; partly to contain the perceived threat of Japanese expansion in Siberia; and partly to be in position to work with Britain and France against the Bolsheviks in the nascent Russian Civil War. Of the some-14,000 US military forces sent to Siberia and the north of Russia, 139 died in fighting and 266 were wounded. The Bolsheviks did not soon forget that the United States had intervened in Russia.

Overall, the United States had made a difference in the Great War and had provided the foundation for bringing it to an end through Wilson's

Fourteen Points, but the ultimate outcome was disastrous. Wilson at one point had called for a "peace without victors" but he found the leaders of Britain, France, and Italy meant to saddle Germany with a Carthaginian peace comprised of a war guilt clause and a massive reparations bill that would undermine the prospects of German democracy in the Weimar Republic and thereby fuel the extreme blowback reaction of Nazism.

Wilson proved unable to sell the Versailles Treaty to the US Senate, which declined to ratify it without changes, thus shattering the president's diplomacy. The League of Nations, which was to anchor peace in the postwar world, would have to limp along without the endorsement of its primary sponsor.

The War at Home

Americans celebrated the allied victory and welcomed home the doughboys, but the war had caused tremendous dislocations in American society. The divisions wrought by the war powerfully influenced the subsequent history of the interwar period, including widespread reluctance to get involved a generation later when a second great war erupted in Europe.

The decision to enter into a foreign war fueled by compulsory military service, at a time when the United States faced no direct threat to its security, spurred a government-orchestrated propaganda campaign to bolster support for the war. Only a year after campaigning on the theme of keeping out of the war, Wilson now declared in June 1917: "Woe be to the man or group of men that seems to stand in our way."

From 1917 to 1919 the Committee on Public Information (CPI) distributed millions of press releases, pamphlets, leaflets, posters, and advertisements to urge all-out support for the war. It mobilized some community leaders and equipped these "Four-Minute Men" with succinct public addresses emphasizing the need for patriotic conformity. They delivered the talks in hundreds of thousands of homes, schools, churches, clubs, community centers, and union halls.

Urged to do their part for the war effort, women and minorities accessed new work opportunities but also weathered reactions against their changing roles in society. Some 367,000 African Americans entered the armed forces, but they were kept in segregated units and relegated to menial positions as common laborers. While some 200,000 African Americans were transported to Europe in the AEF, only a small percentage engaged in combat. Some of those did receive decorations for gallantry—but these were awarded by the French not the US government.

Despite the effort to maintain the Jim Crow system within the US military, African Americans and white men inevitably shared space in training camps, troop ships, and during leaves in France, where the African Americans, Hispanic Americans, and Asian Americans could observe a society in which "colored" people had more social freedom. In the US armed forces only Blacks were segregated, as even Indians--some 12,000 of which served even though they were not considered US citizens--were integrated within the AEF units. Partly on the basis of that service, all Indians were "awarded" US citizenship under a 1924 law.

On the home front, the demand for workers spurred the historic Great Migration of some 750,000 African Americans from the South into northern and western cities. They accessed unprecedented job opportunities but also encountered virulent racist reactions. The influx of African Americans into predominantly white neighborhoods, factories, cities and military training camps ignited a series of vicious race riots killing scores of people, overwhelmingly black, in Chicago, Houston, St. Louis, Tulsa, and other cities.

The war to make the world safe for democracy ironically compelled the United States finally to grant political inclusion to American women, as ratification of the Nineteenth Amendment in 1920 culminated the long struggle for woman's suffrage. Voting rights did not come without a bitter fight to the end, as the National Women's Party had to resort to picketing the White House in wartime, which resulted in more than 200 women being arrested and some force fed in jails amid hunger strikes. Like the racial minorities, thousands of women accessed new work opportunities as a result of the war, but they encountered sexism, wage discrimination, and sexual harassment. While women could not serve in the US military, thousands labored as nurses and clerical and service workers in direct support of the armed forces.

As in subsequent wars, the totalizing focus on mobilizing for the war "over there" brought an end to progressive reform on the home front. Prewar reforms focused on improving American society through direct democracy, a federal income tax, regulation of banking and big business, and rights for workers gave way to the new corporatism and a wave of profiteering fostered by the WIB.

The war brought rising wages and full employment, but inflation and awareness that industries were reaping windfall profits prompted widespread labor unrest and thousands of work stoppages. Business leaders, backed by Wilson, considered efforts to organize labor an affront to patriotic unity in wartime. The administration cracked down against labor movements with propaganda, injunctions, indictments, illegal searches and seizures, strikebreakers, assaults, and arrests.

In the wake of the Bolshevik Revolution, workers and socialists could be demonized by linking them with the communists who had taken Russia out of the war. The reactionary wartime climate combined with the rise of Bolshevism thus provoked the postwar Red Scare targeting of labor activists, immigrants, socialists, and progressive reform.

Civil liberties--as had occurred in the Quasi War, the Civil War, and would materialize again in future American conflicts—suffered serious blows in wartime. Once the United States entered the war, the Wilson administration graduated from propaganda and exhortation to compulsion and retribution.

The Espionage Act of 1917 and the Sedition Act of 1918 undermined freedom of speech and association, enabling prosecution of workers, immigrants, and alleged radicals. The first act gave broad definition to actions considered treasonous or disruptive of the war effort. The Sedition Act outlawed comments viewed as disloyal, even when uttered in private, and even forbade expressions of contempt for the government. Only the Armistice prevented a continuing flood of prosecutions in the worst assault on civil liberties in American history to that point.

Between the Wars

The United States did not "revert" to "isolationism" after the First World War. Despite the rejection of the Versailles Treaty and the League of Nations, the country remained engaged in international diplomacy and continued to grow the military.

In 1920 Congress passed the National Defense Act providing for a professional "Army of the United States" with plans for rapid mobilization of the civilian-based National Guard and civilian reserves in the event of war. Despite the protestations of Mitchell and others, air power remained under the jurisdiction of the Army and the Navy. The Army Air Corps promoted study of air power and training of pilots at Maxwell Field in Alabama while the Navy centered training at the Academy in Annapolis. The Navy acknowledged the growing importance of airpower by converting large cruisers into aircraft carriers.

While the United States continued to improve the quality of its Navy, it also proved willing to negotiate a major international naval arms control accord. In the wake of the Great War, peace internationalists, not "isolationists," demanded arms control, which would save financial resources and reduce the chances of a future war. The United States hosted the negotiations, which produced a series of agreements establishing ratios of tonnage of naval ships as well as a moratorium on building battleships and cruisers. Highly successful, the Washington Naval Conference of

1921-22 brought Japan as well as the European powers into the naval arms control regime. Additional accords recognized respective spheres of influence in East Asia and acknowledged the territorial integrity of China, which had been the target of Western imperialism for decades.

The London Naval Conference of 1930 added follow-up agreements limiting destroyers and submarines, but ominously Japan now rejected the treaties. Increasingly influential Japanese militarists had long been seething over being under greater restraints than the United States and Great Britain—who had justified their higher tonnage ceilings on the basis of operating two-ocean navies while relegating Japan to one—but moreover Japan had embarked on a plan to aggressively expand its sphere of influence in the Asia-Pacific region.

Revivified by the disastrous European war, peace internationalists opposed militarism and tried to outlaw it. In 1928 the United States along with France sponsored the Kellogg-Briand Pact in which more than 60 countries, including Germany, Italy, and Japan renounced war as an instrument of national policy except in the case of self-defense. Throughout the 1920s the United States had also used its economic prosperity to try to stabilize postwar Germany and manage the debt-reparations burden created by the allies at Versailles.

The onset of the Great Depression created global anxiety and insecurities, undermining the effort of peace activists and fueling the rise of extremism and militarism. Over the next few years fascists seized power in Italy and Germany while the militarists took over in Japan. The United States went from the world's economic powerhouse to a desperately struggling nation plagued by record high unemployment and a seemingly insoluble economic crisis.

Nothing better symbolized the pathetic desperation of the times as when in 1932 the Hoover administration ordered the Army to drive out thousands of World War I veterans who had encamped in Anacostia Flats in Washington DC to demand early payment of a bonus promised for their wartime service. The impoverished veterans insisted they needed the money immediately and encamped in a slum of jerry-built "Hoovervilles" when it was not forthcoming. In July, 600 cavalry, tanks, and infantry led by Army Chief of Staff General Douglas MacArthur and including in its ranks the future heroes Majors Dwight D. Eisenhower and George S. Patton, drove out the veterans and burned their hovels to the ground.

Following his landslide election in 1932 Roosevelt tried to promote relief, reform, and recovery in his New Deal, but the initiatives never succeeded in solving the depression.

World War II

After appeasing Nazi Germany's "union" with Austria and its seizure of the Sudetenland of Czechoslovakia at the 1938 Munich Conference, Britain and France pledged to draw the line and to declare war in the event of a German invasion of Poland. The Nazis duly invaded the following year after entering into a pact with the Soviet Union--which desperately sought to fend off or at least delay a German invasion further to the east— on the partition of Poland. The USSR under the dictator Joseph Stalin also reabsorbed the Baltic states, which had been part of the Russian Empire, and invaded Finland.

As with the outbreak of the Great War in 1914, most Americans wanted no part of a second European conflict. The last war clearly had failed to make the world "safe for democracy" and had only left Americans divided against themselves. Furthermore, in the climate fostered by the Depression many Americans embraced the theory that the United States had entered the First World War as a result of the manipulations of bankers and industry elites engaged in war profiteering. From 1934-36 a Senate select committee investigated the charges and, while it found no conspiracy, it did find wartime price fixing, collusion, corruption, and windfall profits among banks and arms manufacturers, dubbed the "merchants of death" in popular accounts. Neutrality legislation designed to keep the United States out of a future war followed and hamstrung the Roosevelt administration's ability to maneuver.

Astute at gauging public opinion, Roosevelt proceeded cautiously in response to the European war, beginning with efforts to shore up American imperialism and reassert the Monroe Doctrine. Despite criticism from peace internationalists, the United States remained an imperial power in the Caribbean and Central America, where it maintained colonies, protectorates and police states reinforced by periodic Marine landings and "gunboat diplomacy." Under Roosevelt's Good Neighbor Policy Washington duly refrained from direct military intervention yet maintained a tight economic grip on Central America and the Caribbean, including continuing efforts to control Mexican resources especially oil. The US State and War Departments bolstered repressive regimes like that of Somoza in Nicaragua as well as Fulgencio Batista in Cuba. Being a "good neighbor" thus did not entail promoting democracy or economic reform, as the United States instead funded and trained the state police forces, enabling them to kill and jail reformers who might challenge the corrupt crony capitalist dictatorships.

Invoking the Monroe Doctrine, Roosevelt shrewdly framed his first major move in favor of the European allies--the destroyers for bases deal with Great Britain in 1940--as an act of hemispheric self-defense rather than foreign intervention. Under the deal the United States received 99-year leases on seven British naval and air bases in the Americas, stretching from Newfoundland to Trinidad, in return for 50 US Navy destroyers. Roosevelt unilaterally extended the Monroe Doctrine to Greenland and Iceland, landing troops on the latter island.

By the time of the destroyers for bases deal the Nazis, led by Adolf Hitler, an embittered and fanatical former World War I foot soldier, had carried out a stunning series of *blitzkrieg* or lightning war attacks on Scandinavia, France and the Low Countries. By June 1940 the Nazis—who had allied with Italy under the fascist dictator Benito Mussolini--had conquered most of Western Europe and were besieging Britain by air.

Most Americans sympathized with Britain and the allies over the Axis powers—which included Japan, which had invaded China and was menacing the entire Pacific world—but many citizens remained leery of direct US involvement. Rival groups—the Committee to Defend America by Aiding the Allies and the America First Committee—squared off in publicity campaigns amid a "great debate" for and against greater US involvement in the conflict. Moving sharply toward increased involvement but not necessarily direct intervention, Roosevelt proposed a program of "lend-lease" aid to the allies in which the United States would supply weapons and materials and thus serve as the "great arsenal of democracy." Numbered as House Resolution 1776 in a blatant appeal to American exceptionalism, the Lend-Lease Act passed the Congress by solid margins in March 1941.

By the time of passage of lend-lease, the Nazis had extended their *blitzkrieg* to overwhelm Greece and Yugoslavia while raining bombs on London, striking the House of Commons. However, Hitler then made the ultimately fatal decision in June 1941 to launch a massive invasion of Eastern Europe and the Soviet Union to fulfill his vision of a 1,000-year Reich. Hitler derived historical inspiration for his plan to dominate and exploit the people and resources of Slavic Europe from the nineteenth-century US conquest of the "red Indians" across the vast American West.

By this time US public support for the allies was growing but Hitler still sought to avoid direct provocation of the United States. Roosevelt, on the other hand, secretly told Churchill at a shipboard conference off the coast of Newfoundland in August 1941 that he would "wage war but not declare it." The two "Anglo-Saxon" leaders pronounced the signing of the Atlantic Charter, a Wilsonian-style document outlining their vision of a free and democratic world.

Weeks later, on September 11, 1941, Roosevelt publicly misrepresented an incident at sea, in which a US destroyer, the *Greer*--engaged in convoying British supply ships--tracked and dropped depth charges on a Nazi submarine. Roosevelt mendaciously asserted that the Nazi "rattlesnakes of the Atlantic" had fired first, whereas in fact the Nazi sub had *responded* with errant torpedo thrusts against the *Greer*.

Like James K. Polk, Lyndon B. Johnson, and George W. Bush, among others, Roosevelt thus deliberately misrepresented an incident to manipulate public opinion in favor of belligerence. Roosevelt exploited the *Greer* incident to authorize an American "shoot on sight" policy, effectively declaring a war at sea. At the time, however, Hitler still sought to avoid war with the United States, leaving Japan to strike the blow that ultimately would bring the Americans directly into the greatest conflagration in world history.

Outbreak of the Pacific War

Efforts to confront Japan's aggressive course in Asia and the Pacific ultimately brought the United States into the Second World War. Put another way, had the United States truly been isolationist, had it chosen not to confront Japan over its aggression thousands of miles from American shores, the Pacific War might not have occurred.

American imperialism had made the nation a Pacific power, one whose military outpost in the Philippines was vulnerable to a rising Japan. Moreover, American missionaries, traders, politicians, and publishers, among others, had long cultivated romanticized attachments to China. Since issuing the Open-Door Notes at the turn of the century, the United States had condemned foreign intervention in China, which remained disunited.

Japanese imperialism in China accelerated with the Twenty-one Demands (1915) followed by the takeover of Manchuria, renamed Manchukuo in 1932. In 1937 Japan launched the Second Sino-Japanese War (the first had been 1894-95), a direct military onslaught into the north of China replete with atrocities and mass killing. A small island nation with outsized ambitions fueled by military fanaticism, Japan sought to exploit the natural resources of China and Southeast Asia to fulfill its own Nazi-like imperial blueprint, the Greater East Asia Co-Prosperity Sphere. In 1940 Japan joined the Tripartite Pact with the Nazis and the Italians. In 1941 Japan invaded Southeast Asia, thus menacing the colonial regimes of Britain, France and Holland.

While the Europeans were rendered powerless by the Nazi onslaught, the United States responded at the end of July by freezing Japanese assets and cutting off its access to oil. Roosevelt put Filipino forces under direct US command and dispatched long-range B-17 bombers to Manila. American intercepts and decoding of Japanese telegraphic communications revealed a desperate regime, unable to pacify the Chinese countryside even as it expanded its imperial overstretch into Indochina, all the while fearing Western "encirclement."

With Roosevelt and Churchill having decided at the Newfoundland conference that war with the Axis was virtually inevitable, the United States rejected negotiations and demanded that Japan "withdraw all military, naval, and police forces from China and Indochina." Japan refused to back down and instead gave a green light to fatally flawed war plans designed to cripple the US fleet in Pearl Harbor, Hawaii.

The United States had not confronted the British, French or Dutch with ultimatums or the cut off of oil supplies as a result of their imperialism, but it would not tolerate Asian imperialism in Asia. In essence, the United States invited rather than doing all that it could to deter further Japanese aggression in the Pacific. On December 7, 1941, Japan launched the stunning surprise attack on the American colony of Hawaii, among other US and European colonial outposts, prompting a swift declaration of war from the United States. US intelligence was aware that Japanese forces were on the move, but the Americans did not anticipate a direct attack on the US imperial outposts while assuming, that if one did occur the Philippines (less than 2,000 miles from Japan) rather than Hawaii (more than 4,000 miles from Japan) would be the likely target. US intelligence intercepts learned of the planned attack on Pearl Harbor just before it took place, but too late to decode, process and pass on the information in time for an alert response.

Hitler responded to the Pearl Harbor attack by abandoning all caution and declaring war on the Americans. Japan's direct attack on American imperial territory and Hitler's ensuing declaration of war on the United States were, along with Hitler's invasion of Russia, utterly disastrous decisions that ultimately sealed the doom of the Axis. Unfortunately, the process of destroying the militarized regimes would take years to accomplish and would result in unprecedented civilian deaths amid the most horrific war in human history. It would also permanently transform the United States into a heavily militarized "superpower."

At the time of Pearl Harbor, unlike previous wars, the United States had an established regular Army ready to be mobilized and a Navy that had been substantially augmented since the collapse of the international naval limitation agreements of the previous decade. American airpower likewise accelerated throughout the 1930s as the United States began long-range patrolling from its bases in Hawaii, the Philippines, and the Panama Canal Zone. By the eve of World War II, the strategic and tactical doctrine encompassing air support for ground operations as well as strategic bombing had become firmly entrenched in Air Corps doctrine.

As the Axis aggression unfolded, Roosevelt stepped up production of new ships, including authorization for 11 new aircraft carriers, as well as 8,000 combat aircraft of various types. Moreover, in the fall of 1940 Roosevelt spurred the Congress to pass the Selective Service and Training Act bringing more than a half million trainees into the army. Masses of Americans remained sharply opposed to compulsory military service, which on this occasion passed by a whisker--203-202 in the House.

The United States was not fully prepared for a two-front global war but it was far more prepared than it had been at the outset of previous American conflicts.

The Sunday morning assault on Hawaii badly damaged but did not cripple the American Pacific fleet. The Japanese destroyed 20 naval vessels, including eight battleships, and some 300 aircraft, but US aircraft carriers were at sea and thus escaped the carnage. The surprise air and naval attack killed some 2,400 people, including civilians, and injured hundreds more.

While the United States had suffered a stunning military blow on its Pacific outposts, including Guam, Wake Island and the Philippines as well as Hawaii, the Japanese assault was nonetheless, perversely, a political bonanza. Virtually overnight it ended the bitterly divisive "great debate" over US intervention, as the nation closed ranks in the wake of the foreign attack on its imperial outposts in the Pacific. As Japanese Admiral Isoroku Yamamoto had anticipated, the Japanese attack would in the end prove far more costly to Japan than to the Americans.

Europe First

The only political problem that remained was that many Americans wanted to focus American firepower on the Japanese aggressors, but US military planning since the late 1930s had committed the nation to a "Europe-first" strategy in the event of a two-front war. The first front of the war for the Americans, as it turned out, was neither Europe nor Asia but rather North Africa. Army generals, including future heroes George C. Marshall and Patton, had wanted to open a second front with an early landing on the European continent—something the Soviet ally, fighting for its survival, also urged—but the US forces were not yet seasoned, fully equipped or adequately mobilized. British Prime Minister Winston Churchill and Roosevelt decided instead on TORCH, the code name for the Anglo-American invasion of Morocco targeting the collaborationist Vichy French regime.

The Grand Alliance between the United States, Britain, and the USSR had been proclaimed and lend-lease aid was flowing to Stalin's regime, but the Red Army was largely left to bear the brunt of the wrath of the Wehrmacht. At a summit in Casablanca in January 1943, Churchill and Roosevelt decided on an invasion of Sicily and Italy while also committing the allies to a policy of "unconditional surrender" in an effort to reassure the Russians that the Western leaders were dedicated to the defeat of Hitler and would eventually bring relief by opening the full-blown second front in Europe. Unconditional surrender sought to ensure that Russia did not leave the war through a separate peace with the Germans, as had occurred in the First World War. The policy also meant the war would be fought all the way to the German capital—and that Soviet troops would be left occupying half of Europe.

The invasion of Sicily in the summer of 1943 helped destabilize Mussolini, whose regime was overthrown, but the Nazi armies initially blunted the Allied offensive. After a bloody fight-- belying Churchill's belief that Italy would prove to be the "soft underbelly of Europe"—the Italians surrendered. Rome fell in June 1944 on the eve of the D-Day landings on the French Normandy coast.

By the time the Allies made their way into the heart of Europe the Soviet Union had already turned back the Nazi armies. After suffering horrific losses in the early stages of the war, the Soviet people to the surprise of many rallied behind the communist regime and prevailed at the epic World War II battle of Stalingrad (Volgograd today) on the banks of the Volga River. The German sixth army suffered devastating losses in the winter battle of 1942-43, which turned the tide of the war and sent the previously invincible Wehrmacht for the first time down to defeat and into retreat.

The Germans were wounded but far from defeated by the time the Western allies launched OVERLORD, the cross-channel invasion orchestrated by General Eisenhower. The June 6 landings succeeded but not without heavy casualties, especially at Omaha Beach. Within weeks more than one million men had been landed in northwestern France, leaving the still powerful Nazi army surrounded on both sides.

By this time the allied strategic bombing was pulverizing German factories, army positions, and ultimately cities and towns. US and British air forces pummeled German positions around the clock but thousands of planes and pilots were lost, especially in the daytime runs anchored mostly by the Americans. US fighter aircraft, however, began to play a critical role in accompanying and defending the B-17 and B-24 bombers. By the end of the war Germany had suffered a saturation bombing unequaled by any other country up to that time in world history—except Japan.

With the Red Army driving to the west and Paris liberated, the Allies began to plot the capture of Berlin. Both the Americans and the Germans suffered heavy casualties in the Battle of the Bulge, as the surprise Nazi counter-offensive in the Ardennes Forest in the final weeks of 1944 was known, but the US forces beat back the offensive and the Allied armies converged on Berlin. At the end of April Hitler shot himself to death in his bunker and the Germans surrendered on May 7.

The Pacific War

While the Soviets bore the primary burden of defeating the Germans, it was the Americans who prevailed over Japan in the Pacific War. The British, to be sure, and other allies played an important supporting role in both major theaters of World War II.

Since the early twentieth century Americans had been war-gaming a potential conflict with Japan. By the 1930s War Plan ORANGE envisioned a conflict in which Japan would overrun US positions, including Guam and the Philippines, in the early stages of a war, requiring the mobilization of US air and naval power to retake the islands, liberate Southeast Asia, and close in on the Japanese home islands. The war in the Pacific in fact unfolded much as ORANGE had envisioned.

The day after Pearl Harbor the Japanese attacked the US imperial outpost in the Philippines which General MacArthur, the Pacific commander, had inexplicably left vulnerable. Scores of aircraft had remained idle at their bases and ripe for destruction even after news of Pearl Harbor had arrived. The United States and the Filipinos subsequently put up a stiff resistance on the island of Corregidor, before it fell to the Japanese.

Japan had driven the British out of Burma, menaced British-controlled India, had isolated Australia, and damaged the US Pacific fleet. Despite these early advantages, and despite the Europe-first strategy, Japan confronted fatal weaknesses. Its military forces were stretched thin across the vast Asia-Pacific region and were bogged down in the interior of China. Moreover, the Pearl Harbor attack had ignited in the American adversary a vindictive fury while firing the engines of what quickly became the most productive war machine in world history. Working around the clock, American factories began to produce war material at a pace that Japanese industry could not hope to match. Japan, in short, had started a war it could not win.

The turning point in the Pacific War came early, in June 1942, at the pivotal battle of Midway. Japan suffered crippling blows in the aircraft carrier battle, losing planes and pilots that it could not readily replace. While British and American forces fought the Japanese to the north in the China-Burma-India theater, MacArthur began a steady northward thrust from Papua New Guinea to the Philippines. American bombers, aircraft carriers and submarines facilitated the amphibious advance, though the island-hopping casualties were dreadful, as in the fighting at the Central Pacific atoll of Tarawa in November 1943.

By 1944 the Japanese were in a death spiral, losing battles to the Americans and moreover losing men, especially pilots and air crews, that could not be replaced. The American victory at Leyte Gulf in October opened the way for MacArthur's celebrated return to the Philippines, a prelude to the planned invasion of Japan's home islands. The Japanese mounted a fanatical resistance, however, fighting to the last man in blood-drenched island battles such as Iwo Jima and Okinawa in the spring of 1945. Having lost most of its well-trained pilots, Japan sent men into the air who could only inflict damage by means of suicidal kamikaze raids slamming their planes into American ships.

Throughout the war American air power exacted a devastating toll in Japan. Distinctions between civilian and military targets eroded completely, as in the firebombing of Tokyo in March, which incinerated 84,000 people. By June American airpower had virtually de-urbanized Japan and killed some 900,000 civilians. Memories of Pearl Harbor, demonization of the Japanese in American popular culture as ape-like subhuman creatures, and the dictates of unconditional surrender ("slap the Jap off the map") fueled what scholars have called a "war without mercy" replete with indiscriminate killing.

The atomic bombings of Hiroshima and Nagasaki on Aug. 6 and 9 thus reflected a continuous policy of mass slaughter that had already been occurring, not only in Japan but in air raids on German cities such as Dresden, Hamburg, and Berlin as well. The technology of the new weapon was novel in its destructive capacity, to be sure, but the atomic bombs merely did better what had already been occurring.

The United States had developed the atomic bomb through a well-orchestrated (except for its penetration by Soviet spies) scientific research program, and it meant to use them, reasoning no doubt accurately that Japan or Germany would have done the same to them. US officials later invented inflated figures as to the number of Americans who would have died without the atomic bombings, though beyond question an invasion of the home islands, if it had come to that, would have entailed heavy casualties on both sides. But Japan was already defeated by the time of the atomic bombings and a diplomatic understanding—which the United States ultimately had to agree to even after Hiroshima and Nagasaki—in which the Emperor Hirohito was allowed to retain the throne as a strictly ceremonial figure bereft of power might have been entered into and thus ended the war sooner. No one can say for sure, however, what could have happened; what can be said for sure is that the war ended and the nuclear age dawned.

Warfare would never be the same again, as the usage of a weapon of unparalleled destructive power capped off by far the most destructive war—especially in terms of civilian deaths—in human history. The United States suffered about 1.7 million casualties in World War II, including more than 400,000 deaths, 291,000 of those dying on the battlefield. These horrific casualties could not compare, however, to other belligerents, especially the USSR, which suffered about 27 million dead. Germany lost some seven million dead and Japan about three million, terrible figures, yet these aggressor states caused far more death than they suffered. All told, some 75 million people died, including as many as 20 million in China as a result of Japan's aggression. Among the tens of millions killed as a result of Nazi aggression were six million Jews and other minorities, who were slaughtered in the Nazi genocide.

The Homefront

As in the First World War and other major conflicts in US history, World War II dramatically changed American society. Of utmost significance, the war brought an end to the worst economic collapse in American history. Militarism thus brought full employment and a skyrocketing Gross Domestic Product that carried over into an era of postwar prosperity. The war permanently ensconced the military-industrial complex, with profound implications for US history and society.

For women and minorities, the second world war like the first one was a tremendous engine of change. Women remained excluded from the draft and from a combat role but some 333,000 served in uniform overseas in auxiliary services, including life-saving work in the nursing and medical fields. At home, women in large numbers entered into factory and industrial jobs from which they were previously barred, as wartime propaganda urged "Rosie the Riveter" to play a central role in wartime production, which she did. The war and postwar prosperity paved the way for women to enter into colleges and universities in unprecedented numbers; to begin to access professional fields like law and medicine previously overwhelmingly dominated by men; and decades later to orchestrate the second wave of the women's movement, advancing an ongoing quest for equality.

African Americans served and fought in segregated units, but for the last time: in 1948 President Harry Truman terminated segregation of the armed forces by executive order. Truman thus honored previously marginalized African American military service for the first time in US history. Blacks were drafted and overall some 125,000 served during World War II, again mostly in subsidiary roles reflecting the white supremacy that prevailed throughout the largely segregated American society. The most celebrated African American fighters were the Tuskegee (Alabama) airmen, an all-black fighter squadron that fought with distinction in the Mediterranean theater. Some African Americans merited Medals of Honor for their wartime service, but the military followed an unwritten policy of not granting them to blacks. Some were awarded decades later.

As many as a half a million Hispanics served in World War II, though most headlines were reserved for the home front when young Hispanic men clashed with whites as well as the Los Angeles police in the so-called "Zoot-suit riots" of 1943. Some 25,000 Native Americans fought in the war, including the famous Navaho "wind talkers" who served as signal callers in the Pacific by supplying a language that Japanese code breakers failed to comprehend.

More than 30,000 Japanese Americans fought in World War II even as some 120,000 first- and second-generation Americans of Japanese ancestry, more than half of them US citizens, had their property confiscated and were deported to War Relocation Authority Centers—barb-wire enclosed prison camps—dotted across the American West. In 1988 the US Government formally apologized and compensated survivors for this gross violation of civil liberties. Some German- and Italian Americans were interned as well during the war, but on a much smaller scale.

World War II was the greatest conflagration in history, transforming virtually every country on the globe, including the United States. Perceived as a "good war" by the Americans because it had ended in unambiguous victory and delivered economic prosperity as well, World War II nonetheless cast an ominous shadow over the succeeding era.

Chapter 6
Waging Wars Cold and Hot

Providentially sanctioned American exceptionalism was riding high in the wake of unambiguous victory in the two-front world war. The Great Depression was just a bad memory, as the United States had achieved full economic recovery through wartime production and now possessed preponderant global economic influence. The US dollar was the world's preeminent currency while the World Bank and the International Monetary Fund, along with the new United Nations, were US-based and US-dominated. The United States had a Navy and an Air Force second to none and sole possession of the atomic bomb.

Clearly the most powerful nation in the world, the United States embarked on a quest to fulfill publisher Henry Luce's vision of an "American century" dominated by liberal capitalist internationalism. It was Manifest Destiny all over again, but this time on a global rather than merely a continental scale.

The nation expanded imperialism as it sought to extract resources while implanting "the American way of life" around the world. The United States fortified military bases worldwide and intervened militarily in previously unimaginable locations, including fighting a major war on the Korean Peninsula.

The federally directed military-industrial complex, germinated in the Civil War, expanded in World War I, was now permanently ensconced in the wake of the Second World War. The military branches as well as private "defense" industries had accumulated power and prestige during the war and would not allow their resources and positions to diminish. Interservice rivalry propelled increased influence over Congress and growth of all the service branches.

In 1947 the National Security Act reorganized the US military bureaucracy, beginning with the establishment of the Air Force as a fourth military branch. The legislation also created the Joint Chiefs of Staff comprised of the commanders of each military branch reporting to a civilian secretary of the newly created Department of Defense, which replaced the War Department.

The National Security Council (NSC) was created to draft policy papers and advise the president on the new global foreign policy. The Central

Intelligence Agency, whose director sat on the NSC, replaced the wartime Office of Strategic Services and was charged with intelligence gathering as well as "psychological warfare" operations worldwide. These agencies emphasized secrecy, as the public's right to know eroded sharply in the postwar era.

This metastasizing "national security state" was inextricably linked with the Cold War. The Grand Alliance with the Soviet Union had served its purpose, as the Soviets had done the overwhelming bulk of the dying in World War II—some 27 million deaths, well more than 50 times the number the United States suffered.

As a result of the deliberate allied wartime strategy, the Soviet Red Army occupied half of the European continent, as well as other areas of the world, at the war's end. Though devastated by the war with the Nazis, the USSR was nonetheless positioned to exert unprecedented influence in the wake of the conflict. Now that the war was over, the United States reverted to vilification of the "godless communist" regime. Americans wanted no competition from radical regimes in their quest to lead the world.

The United States and its allies thus lacked the realism to accept, while trying to manage or limit, the inevitability of expanded Soviet influence as a result of the wartime triumph and sacrifices endured by the USSR. Here the shift from the more flexible Roosevelt to the inexperienced and woefully provincial Truman made a difference. With the United States and Great Britain taking the lead, Western enmity for the USSR and communist ideology escalated dramatically after the war.

The intensely anti-communist State Department had chafed over the wartime alliance with the Stalin regime, which in the 1930s had slaughtered millions of people in a forced collectivization and industrialization campaign. Stalin had also orchestrated show trials and executions including former heroes of the Bolshevik Revolution in order to solidify his monopoly on political power. In February 1946 George F. Kennan, a State Department diplomat long posted in the USSR, dispatched the famous "long telegram," which he followed up with an anonymously published article in *Foreign Affairs*. Kennan condemned the Soviet regime and advocated a confrontational policy of deploying measures short of war--a new policy of "containment" in place of the wartime alliance and international collaboration.

In March Churchill, deposed as British prime minister but still idolized in the United States, declared in a famous speech in Truman's home state of Missouri, with the president beaming alongside on the stage, that the Soviet regime had erected an "iron curtain" across the European continent. Stalin condemned the speech as reactionary and condemned capitalism and Western imperialism as well. Rather than providing Russia with loans and compensation for its massive sacrifices in the war, as Roosevelt had promised, the Western powers were reverting to confrontation.

In March 1947 the United States affirmed the emerging Cold War with the assertion of the Truman Doctrine, a military assistance program to Greece and Turkey. Truman's pronouncement, clearly aimed at the USSR, contained the universalist pledge to offer military aid throughout the world to "free peoples who are resisting subjugation by armed minorities or by outside pressures." In reality the Greek and Turkish regimes were authoritarian rather than democratic. The US support for "free peoples" was empty rhetoric: the Truman Doctrine sanctioned decades of US military assistance to right-wing regimes as long as they were anti-communist. Making the world "safe for democracy" was mere window-dressing and not an actual priority.

The Truman administration also initiated the European Recovery Program, or Marshall Plan, which succeeded through loans and assistance in revivifying the economies of war-ravaged Europe. The loans helped restore confidence and stimulated trade and political ties between the United States and Western Europe. Instead of making genuine efforts to include the Soviet Union, the recovery program was framed in such a way as to alienate the communist regime, thereby achieving its aim of prompting the USSR to withdraw from the talks and cementing the Cold War divide. With the western European nations coalescing as an economic bloc linked with the United States, Stalin clamped down on Eastern Europe, making Churchill's iron curtain more of a reality than it had been.

Stalin had not moved immediately to communize all of Eastern Europe, but as the Grand Alliance collapsed, he and his red allies in the emerging East bloc began to do so. The Soviets forced Czechoslovakia out of the Paris talks on the Marshall Plan, followed by the death of liberal leader Jan Masaryk. The events in Czechoslovakia reminded people of Hitler's aggression precipitating appeasement at Munich. The Western nations decried appeasement and vowed to confront the Soviets.

The division of Germany into two regimes, replete with a war scare in Berlin in 1948, solidified the new Cold War and along with it the militarization of American foreign policy for decades to come. With diplomacy at a standstill, the United States further solidified the divide with the creation of an anti-communist military alliance directed at the Soviet Union.

Deep-seated principles of US foreign policy, first propounded by George Washington, affirmed by the Monroe Doctrine, and holding steady until the First World War had been abandoned. No longer avoiding "entangling alliances," the United States would instead cultivate allies around the world to facilitate a new globalized foreign policy of anti-communist containment. The new CIA carried out covert operations, including funneling millions of dollars to undermine the Communist Party in elections in Italy in 1948.

In 1949, with the support of the Joint Chiefs and the new Defense Department, the United States promulgated the North Atlantic Treaty Organization (NATO) with the nations of Western Europe. Authorized under the Article 51 provision of "collective self-defense" under the UN Charter, NATO declared that an attack on one nation would trigger a collective response.

In reality there was no threat of Soviet aggression. Stalin was a brutal dictator but unlike Hitler he was not a reckless aggressor. Ravaged by the war, the USSR had no intention, rationale or prospect of launching a *blitzkrieg* attack on Western Europe. Vivid memories of Hitler, however, combined with the need to "scare the hell out of the country," as one US senator put it, in order to gain support for the new national security regime, propelled an 82-13 affirmative vote in the Senate resolution that enabled creation of the US-led alliance.

Rather than the ostensible purpose of deterring Soviet aggression, NATO functioned to fortify the economic and security arrangements between Western Europe and the United States. At the same time, the alliance cemented a division of Europe and much of the rest of the world between capitalist and communist blocs. In late August 1949, the successful Soviet test of an atomic weapon, hastened by espionage, increased Western fears. The near simultaneous triumph of communism in the civil war that had been raging in China stunned the Americans and deepened the global divide.

Lurching into panic mode in the wake of the "fall" of China, US national security elites committed the nation to a policy of unbounded global intervention. The psychology of the Cold War was such that Americans feared that the loss of *any* country—no matter how small or strategically insignificant—could create a stampede that eventually would undermine liberal capitalism and the United States itself.

This theory of falling dominoes was a recipe for American global imperialism, which duly followed. The United States invariably depicted intervention in defensive terms, namely "containment" and support for the "free world" against "communist aggression," but in actuality US actions were often aggressive, imperial and in support of right-wing regimes.

The Cold War began in Europe but quickly went global. At its very essence the Cold War entailed indirect conflict between the great powers. However, the actual fighting and dying most directly affected people on the periphery in the so-called Third World where the ideological struggle between communism and capitalism was waged.

Scores of new nations sought national independence after being dominated by European imperialism since the latter half of the nineteenth century. They had been inspired by the World War II defeat of fascism and the UN's Universal Declaration of Human Rights in 1948. In many countries, leftists embraced Marxist-Leninist condemnation of Western imperialism while others professed neutralism. The Soviet Union and China supported leftist movements while the United States in the Truman Doctrine gave military support to virtually any regime that was non-communist.

Choosing War in Korea

Much of Asia, like Europe, was left divided at the end of the war. The Korean Peninsula proved the most combustible spot in the aftermath of the Pacific War. After declaring war on Japan on August 8, 1945, the Soviet Union moved troops into northeastern Korea. A week later, with the war now over, Truman and Stalin agreed to divide the former Japanese colony at the 38th parallel. As with Germany the division was intended to be temporary, as Korea was ethnically homogeneous and for centuries had been a unified state.

As the Cold War unfolded, the occupations became ensconced in the north under the Soviet-backed communist Kim Il-sung and in the south under the US-backed authoritarian Syngman Rhee. In 1948 the Soviet Union ended its postwar military occupation and the United States reciprocated the following year. However, both countries continued to supply weapons and retain military advisers on the ideologically divided peninsula.

Long established as an imperial power in the Asia-Pacific region, the United States bolstered its bases in the Philippines, which received formal independence in 1946 but remained firmly in the American orbit through political and security arrangements secured by nearly a half century of occupation. The Americans occupied and dominated postwar Japan, where military bases were constructed and expanded notably at Okinawa.

Reeling over the "loss" of China, the United States determined to ensure that *all* Southeast Asia would remain anti-communist. Washington thus arrogated to itself the protean task of directing the economic, political and security orientations of an array of countries across a vast landed and maritime region of the world. Adoption of the global containment policy transformed previously insignificant countries--like Korea and Vietnam--into vital proving grounds.

As conflict escalated in Korea, both Kim and Rhee liquidated political opponents and demanded the right to unite the entire peninsula under

95

their own authority. Kim repeatedly sought Stalin's approval to launch a major military assault on the south, for which he eventually received a green light. "Red China" was not consulted prior to the attack launched by Kim's forces on June 25, 1950, which ignited the full-blown Korean War.

As Kim rejected a UN Security Council demand for withdrawal, Seoul fell to the invaders from the north. At that point the Truman administration decided with minimal discussion and almost no dissent that, absent US intervention, the "credibility" of the global anti-communist containment policy would suffer a crippling blow. American Century exceptionalism, the domino theory, and the legacies of appeasement at Munich combined to spur direct US intervention.

The United States thus decided that its "national security" required it to intervene militarily on an Asian peninsula 6,000 miles from American shores. Such a decision would have been unthinkable in 1940, underscoring the extent to which the world and US foreign and military policy had been completely transformed by World War II and the Cold War.

Atrocities materialized on the first day of fighting, as for three days beginning on June 25 US forces strafed and machine-gunned innocent Korean refugees, killing hundreds of mostly women and children fleeing for their lives at No Gun Ri. The massacre remained secret until 1999. More evidence surfaced thereafter of deliberate attacks on refugees, as an indiscriminate war unfolded on the Korean Peninsula.

The United States unleashed air and naval attacks, including B-29 bombings of North Korean supply lines as well as civilian and industrial targets extending to Pyongyang. The first wave of US intervention could not stop the southward thrust of North Korean forces. The US Eighth Army clung to the Pusan Perimeter in the far southeastern corner of the Korean peninsula while awaiting the broader mobilization of US forces.

On July 7, 1950, the UN Security Council authorized use of military force under the command of the United States to repel the northern Korean aggression. The Soviet Union could have vetoed the resolution had it not been boycotting the UN over its unrealistic recognition of the loser of the civil war, the Republic of China (Taiwan), rather than the People's Republic as the legitimate government of China. Now thoroughly politicized under US domination, the UN, which was supposed to function as a catalyst of international peace and cooperation, became an early casualty of the Cold War.

The outbreak of the Korean War confirmed the heavily militarized global imperial policy, which took on the character of a crusade against evil with Truman's signature on NSC 68 (1950). The policy paper, which remained classified for 25 years, depicted the global Cold War as a life-or-death struggle between freedom and communist "slavery." It authorized a massive increase in defense spending, including development of virtually any new weapons system that could be devised, beginning with a green light for incorporating into the American arsenal the thermonuclear or hydrogen bomb.

Truman gave General MacArthur, the Pacific War hero who had overseen the initial postwar occupation of Japan, broad authority to pursue the Korean War as he saw fit. MacArthur decided on a risky amphibious landing at the west coast port city of Inchon, which he carried off successfully in mid-September. Before the month ended Seoul had been liberated and the bombing runs had begun to disrupt North Korean supply lines. The Eighth Army stormed out of the Pusan Perimeter and began to propel the invaders back to the north.

At the time, the victory on two fronts in World War II still cast an aura of American invincibility, lulling MacArthur and the nation in general into an intoxicating state of overconfidence. The Truman administration-- under brutal political attack from the "Asia-first" right-wing for the "loss" of China--craved a decisive victory over communism to silence predominantly Republican critics who assailed containment as a defensive and even "pantywaist" strategy.

In October, as the US/UN forces approached the Yalu River dividing China and North Korea, MacArthur pledged that the troops would be "home by Christmas." In early November, however, masses of "Red" Chinese forces assisted by Soviet-made MIG fighters intervened. The Truman administration had ignored warnings from India, which was acting as an intermediary because the United States did not recognize or speak with communist China, that Mao Zedong would intervene if hostile forces continued the march toward China's southern border.

All that would have been required for a realistic "intelligence" assessment would have been to imagine what the United States might have done had hostile forces that refused to recognize its legitimacy or existence been marching an army north through Mexico and approached the Rio Grande. In such a scenario the United States undoubtedly would have launched a massive preemptive military strike.

At the end of November, as waves of Chinese troops stormed into Korea, MacArthur acknowledged that "an entirely new war" had dawned. The Americans were forced into an ignominious retreat, leaving weapons and equipment behind in their desperation. Lasting until mid-December, it became the longest military retreat in US history.

In the first week of the new year Seoul fell once again to the Chinese-backed North Korean invaders. US forces rallied, however, and retook Seoul in a March counteroffensive, at which point the Korean War assumed the enduring characteristics of a blood-drenched stalemate.

MacArthur demanded an armistice and vowed to unleash an attack on mainland China if the communists refused to end the fighting. A presidential aspirant, MacArthur leaked his threat of a wider war with China to his Republican colleagues at home.

In April 1951 Truman, backed by the JCS, sacked MacArthur for insubordination and the blatant challenge to civilian authority over military policy. Congressional hearings and condemnation of Truman ensued, but in reality, the American public lacked enthusiasm for an all-out land war in Asia with the most populous country in the world, one whose leaders were willing to sacrifice hundreds of thousands of lives to oppose the imperialist invaders.

The Korean War would teach many lessons to those willing to learn them. While the United States had widely perceived a monolithic communist menace endangering the world, the communist world had in fact been disunited from the start, as reflected in the break and near war in 1948 between Stalin and the Yugoslav communist regime led by Marshal Josip Broz Tito. Despite a Soviet-Chinese alliance forged in 1950, Stalin and Kim had not even informed Mao's China in advance of the northern Korean attack of June 1950. In the wake of US intervention, Stalin wanted to avoid war with the Americans whereas Mao plunged into one, reaping the approbation of the "Third World" anti-imperialist movement as a result.

Rather than functioning as puppets, the North Koreans and the South Koreans plagued their sponsors with unilateral decision-making and extreme stubbornness. Throughout the history of the Cold War, the supposedly weaker "proxy" states actually exerted significant influence and often pulled the strings over their supposed great power puppet masters.

By the early months of 1951 the Korean War had become a stalemate, which all of the major powers sought to contain in order to avoid a general war in an atomic-weapons equipped world. However, neither Kim nor Rhee wanted to settle for anything short of full control of the peninsula. Thus, the war continued.

While negotiations achieved little progress, the Korean War took on the character of a senseless conflict reminiscent of the trench warfare in World War I. Otherwise meaningless sites like Pork Chop Hill and Bloody Ridge changed hands in repeated gut-wrenching fights. The United States continued to pummel Korea from the air, killing hundreds of thousands of people and causing masses of civilian casualties. The Korean War remained atrocity filled on both sides.

While the armistice talks stymied, ostensibly over the contentious issue of repatriation of prisoners, the real issue was that neither Rhee nor Kim wanted to settle for a draw. With the death of Stalin and a new administration in Washington demanding an end to the war in 1953, the armistice talks gained momentum. Bitter at not getting control of Korea, Rhee freed 30,000 North Korean prisoners in an effort to sabotage the talks, but with the war hopelessly stalemated the signing of the armistice finally came off in July 1953. Divided at the start, Korea remained divided at the finish, separated by a demilitarized zone that endures as one of the most-tense borders in the world today.

The United States suffered more than 37,000 dead and more than 100,000 wounded in Korea, a fraction of what the Koreans and the Chinese suffered. While China had more than a million casualties, Koreans suffered the most. With its rapidly changing fronts and the punishing American bombing, North and South Korea combined suffered more than four million casualties, as some 10 percent of the Korean civilian population lay dead in the so-called "limited war."

North Korea reverted to the "hermit kingdom" past as it devolved into a warped and repressive Kim family dictatorship. South Korea was a US imperial outpost and an authoritarian militarist regime for decades. In 1980 the US-backed South Korean military dictatorship brutally repressed an uprising at Gwangju, killing hundreds of pro-democracy protesters, but the movement persisted and triumphed in 1987 with the transition to free elections. South Korea has been a high-functioning democracy ever since. It remains a militarized US imperial outpost.

The combination of the Cold War and decolonization had proven highly combustible in Korea. The Korean War was the pivot into a supposedly "cold" war era that in fact featured many highly destructive "hot" shooting wars. As the superpowers armed and equipped rival forces across Asia, Africa, and Latin America, they kept the violence centered on the darker-skinned peoples of the developing countries and away from their own shores.

Militarization Trumps Reform

Sometimes viewed as the "forgotten war," as it has been overshadowed by the "good war" of World War II and disastrous Vietnam conflict, the Korean War was in reality highly consequential for the United States as well as the rest of the world. As the defense budget soared to new heights, the United States made permanent the military bases in Japan and South Korea, redoubled the commitment to containment throughout Southeast Asia (including the obscure country of Vietnam), and positioned the Seventh Fleet in the Taiwan Straits, thus ensuring lasting US involvement in the conflict between Taiwan and mainland China.

As in World War I, the United States ushered in a renewal of red scare politics and repression of civil liberties that peaked during the Korean War. The global crusade against communism and the espionage-assisted and thus earlier than expected Soviet possession of the atomic bomb spurred a witch-hunt atmosphere in American domestic politics.

Conservatives hamstrung Truman's Fair Deal, as the New Deal legacy of domestic reform was demonized as creeping socialism and forced into retreat. Militarization and security reigned as J. Edgar Hoover's FBI orchestrated a highly consequential purge of the left from American political life. "Containment" unfolded at home as well as abroad as the forces of reaction repressed advocates of racial equality, feminists, and non-heterosexuals, who were persecuted as deviants.

Socialists and communists were driven out of American political life. A series of highly publicized postwar FBI and congressional investigations targeted leftists including the "Hollywood Ten," State Department diplomat Alger Hiss, and former Vice President Henry A. Wallace, among many others. The virulent antics of Senator Joe McCarthy (R-WI) incited widespread public fears of what he called a "vast communist conspiracy" to infiltrate and topple the US Government. A federal judge ordered the execution of Julius Rosenberg, who had been a civilian engineer in the US Army Signal Corps, following conviction for passing atomic secrets to the Soviets. On June 19, 1953 Rosenberg and his wife Ethel, also convicted of conspiracy to commit espionage, were both executed by electric chair (the first attempt to kill Mrs. Rosenberg failed), orphaning their two children.

The trial and execution of the Rosenbergs was the most sensational event in a generalized assault on American communism (both Julius and Ethel had been Communist Party members). Hoover's FBI systematically tracked down former communists and alleged radicals for investigation and persecution compromising their jobs and families regardless of whether they remained active in left-wing politics.

As a result of the purge, in the wake of World War II and the Cold War American politics effectively began at the center and moved to the right. Unlike Western Europe, where national health care and other social reforms took place, the United States contained the left on the home front while acting as a militarized imperial power abroad.

The hunt for "atom spies" heightened anxiety over the dawning of the nuclear age, which was powerfully and ubiquitously symbolized by depictions of the atomic mushroom cloud. Both Truman and his successor, President Dwight D. Eisenhower, elected in 1952, threatened to use nuclear weapons to bring an end to the fighting in Korea, but it became apparent that the ultimate weapon had little practical application on the battlefield. A decision to use the bomb could lead to a self-destructive all-out nuclear war with the Soviet Union. Moreover, as the

Prussian military theorist Clausewitz had explained in the previous century, war was but the continuation of politics by other means. Nuclear weapons could kill masses of people, to be sure, but they could not change "hearts and minds." Mass killing could not resolve a civil-ideological conflict such as the war in Korea, or the many other Cold War conflicts that emerged after World War II.

The United States fueled the nuclear arms race, authorizing first the hydrogen or fusion bomb and thereafter virtually every other innovation the lavishly funded atomic scientists and their sponsors could imagine. Despite the bomb's limitations, Eisenhower and his Secretary of State John Foster Dulles centered their "New Look" diplomacy around the threat to unleash "massive retaliation" as a means of deterring communist expansion. A Republican fiscal conservative, Eisenhower deplored the massive defense spending spawned by NSC 68 and the Korean conflict. Nuclear weapons provided "more bang for the buck" than conventional defense strategy, which required the commitment of large military forces overseas. Eisenhower and Dulles discovered, however, that the threat of nuclear retaliation proved feckless in deterring communist-inspired "wars of national liberation." The Eisenhower administration considered but ultimately rejected using nuclear weapons against both the Vietminh, as they overran the French base at Dienbienphu in 1954 (see next chapter), as well as "Red China," as it shelled the offshore islands Quemoy and Matsu in the ongoing conflict with Taiwan in 1954 and again in 1958.

The US Air Force capitalized on the New Look emphasis on massive retaliation, as the Strategic Air Command (SAC) developed the capacity to deliver nuclear weapons, especially following the introduction in 1955 of the B-52 intercontinental bomber. The development of the strategic triad, in which nuclear warheads could be launched from air, land or sea, enabled all the services to get a hand in the American-led nuclear arms race. While the Air Force developed the Thor intermediate range missile, the Army cultivated the land-based Jupiter missiles, and the Navy's Polaris program featured mobile and thus virtually invulnerable nuclear-powered submarines.

The Soviet launch of Sputnik in October 1957 created the biggest nationwide panic since the fall of China, fueling the military-industrial complex that later prompted a pointed warning from Eisenhower as he left office. The satellite launch showed that the Soviets could reach the United States with intercontinental ballistic missiles (ICBM), yet there was no "missile gap" as proclaimed by rival politicians and the self-promoting military-industrial complex. Americans retained strategic superiority. Nonetheless, the Sputnik-inspired panic produced congressional hearings and grave reports of vulnerability, which spurred unprecedented levels of "defense" spending.

The fallout from the artificial Sputnik crisis led to construction of backyard bomb shelters and passage of the National Defense Education Act, which increased funding for mathematics and science education on the premise that "Johnny" had fallen dangerously behind "Ivan" in these areas. In addition, Congress passed the Defense Reorganization Act providing the Secretary of Defense greater civilian command over the Joint Chiefs of Staff and the rival military services.

Eisenhower left office issuing the historic warning against the "unwarranted influence" of the burgeoning military-industrial complex. The hero president explained that the Cold War obsession with weapons and "national security" had created a powerful constituency that exercised excessive influence over policy. He lamented the "insidious penetration of our own minds that the only thing this country is engaged in is weaponry and missiles." The "potential for the disastrous rise of misplaced power exists and will persist." These prescient warnings would be ignored.

Eisenhower left a mixed legacy on militarization—which he had both escalated and condemned—but there was nothing ambiguous about the administration's emphasis on covert operations, including CIA coups as well as assassination plots. Eisenhower and the Dulles brothers— Secretary of State John Foster and CIA Director Allen Dulles—were enamored with waging psychological warfare, including radio propaganda beamed behind the "iron curtain," as well as conducting covert operations. Through Radio Free Europe and other aggressive "psywar" operations the United States sought to undermine communism in Eastern Europe, but these actions served only to harden the regimes and when necessary, as in Hungary in 1956 and Czechoslovakia in 1968, prompt direct Soviet intervention. "Liberation," trumpeted as an alternative to the "weak" policy of containment, was much ballyhooed and yet in practical terms an abject failure.

Under Eisenhower the CIA became the spearhead of American imperialism in the Third World. In 1953 the CIA, working with the British, launched a secret coup (Operation Ajax) that overthrew the elected government of Iran after the prime minister Mohammad Mossadegh moved toward a partial nationalization of Iranian oil. The move threatened a gigantic British refinery and US corporate oil interests. A charismatic leader, Mossadegh was determined to decolonize Iran. Though non-communist himself, Mossadegh tolerated the Tudeh, the Iranian communist party.

The Anglo-American-backed coup entailed a range of tactics including assassination, demonstrations, and payoffs culminating in a military assault. Mossadegh was jailed and replaced by an authoritarian regime backed by a repressive secret police force and led by a pro-Western monarch, Shah Reza Pahlavi. Western oil interests were secured. The

Iranian intervention, coupled with the cultivation of the reactionary Saudi Arabian monarchy, underscored that access and profits from oil were far more important than promoting democracy in the "free world." In sum, Western imperialism trumped democracy and decolonization.

Thrilled with the success of the imperial takeover in Iran, Eisenhower and the CIA in 1954 orchestrated another "successful" coup against the left-wing reform government of Jacobo Arbenz in the small Central American country of Guatemala. There the United States empowered a vicious military regime that would kill and imprison tens of thousands of people, all with the backing and support of the leader of the "free world." Similarly, in January 1961 CIA operatives colluded with Belgian colonialists and right-wing militants in the Congo in the overthrow and murder of reform leader Patrice Lumumba.

The New Frontier

Eisenhower's successor, Massachusetts Senator John. F. Kennedy, who narrowly prevailed in the 1960 election, was an ardent cold warrior but a critic of the New Look. A gifted orator, Kennedy invoked the romanticized history of American exceptionalism as he spoke of a "new frontier" and pledged in his inaugural to "pay any price, bear any burden" in waging the Cold War.

Kennedy and others feared that the United States was losing the Third World in the struggle against communism. As decolonization movements flourished, the European empires—including the French, Dutch, Belgian, and British—quickly receded as scores of new nations emerged across Asia and Africa. At the Bandung Conference in 1955, Third World leaders including the host, Indonesian President Sukarno, as well as Prime Minister Jawaharlal Nehru of India, advocated non-alignment or neutralism in the Cold War.

Third World leaders and much of their publics condemned the long American history of internal colonialism and white supremacy. The Eisenhower administration, however, sympathized with the white European colonizers. Eisenhower feared that African decolonization, which unfolded rapidly following the independence of Sudan (1956) and Ghana (1957), would unleash "primitive savagery" and instability that could be exploited by the USSR to promote communism. African Americans, however, empowered in the wake of their participation in World War II, spearheaded the burgeoning civil rights movement in the American South and championed African decolonization.

US officials strove to contain the black reformers in Africa as well as those on the home front. Hoover's FBI spied upon and harassed the

Council on African Affairs and other left-wing groups that identified with the African diaspora. Radical and socialist African American leaders such as Paul Robeson and W.E.B. DuBois—like radicals and socialists generally—were condemned and repressed after World War II.

Ironically, the international pressures of the Cold War ultimately spurred the more mainstream civil rights movement within the United States. In 1957, three years after the historic Brown v. Board of Education decision in the US Supreme Court, virulent American racism was captured by television cameras and displayed worldwide amid the tumult of the Little Rock, Arkansas, desegregation crisis. Eisenhower reluctantly ordered the National Guard to enforce the high court decision on school integration. National security elites feared that the overseas image of the "ugly American," racist in his own land and indifferent to Third World concerns, would discredit the global effort to contain communism. By the early 1960s the civil rights movement could no longer be repressed.

Relentless protests spearheaded by Martin Luther King, Jr., among others, brought historic civil rights reforms ending segregation and establishing de jure voting rights for African Americans, but the United States, as the Kerner Commission (1968) concluded, remained "two societies, one black, one white—separate and unequal." The civil rights movement did not translate abroad in the mid-1960s, as the United States, fearful of "black power" at home as well as abroad, continued to embrace the apartheid and militarist African regimes.

In contrast to Eisenhower, Kennedy criticized European colonialism as he tried to improve US standing with non-white peoples in the developing world. Kennedy broke with France over its bloody repression of Algerian independence. The United States had previously backed the claim that Algeria was a legitimate French settler state rather than a colonized North African nation. France acquiesced to the independence of Morocco and Tunisia but waged a brutal yet ultimately failed counterinsurgency war that killed about a million people in Algeria from 1956-62.

Kennedy did not, however, challenge US imperial policies in the Congo, South Africa, and many other African countries. In the Congo the charismatic Lumumba had inherited the legacies of the extraordinarily brutal history of Belgian colonization. He charted a reform course that included "positive neutrality" in the Cold War and the withdrawal of Belgian military forces. Neither provision was acceptable to the United States or its European ally, which variously condemned the progressive reformer as "erratically irresponsible," a "sorcerer," and a "red weed." Allen Dulles declared Lumumba's "removal must be an urgent and prime objective," but Belgian troops and Congolese opponents beat the CIA to the punch, as they tortured and then executed Lumumba in January 1961.

Receiving the new dictator of the Congo, General Joseph Mobutu at the White House in 1963, Kennedy declared, "Nobody in the world had done more than the General to maintain freedom against the communists." Mobutu ruled the Congo (which he renamed Zaire) as an autocrat for more than three decades during which time he plundered the country of billions of dollars accrued to his personal wealth while jailing and often executing critics and political opponents.

Bowing to the esteemed "wise man" and former secretary of state Dean Acheson's advice not to "pander to the dark and delirious continent of Africa," Kennedy maintained US support for the anti-communist white supremacist regimes in South Africa and Rhodesia. South Africa was the world's leading gold supplier and a strategic Cold War ally. Both regimes enforced legally mandated racial separation.

Nelson Mandela, the founder of the African National Congress, like Lumumba was not a communist but rather a social reformer who demanded an end to South African apartheid. The United States joined South Africa in condemning the ANC as a communist front group, leading to the trial and conviction of Mandela for subversion. Washington expressed its approval as Mandela was lodged in prison, where he would spend the next 27 years.

In addition to the concern about losing the Third World, Kennedy's New Frontier condemned Eisenhower's New Look for its obsessive focus on nuclear weapons and massive retaliation. Kennedy implemented "flexible response" under which the United States continued to cultivate a massive arsenal of nuclear missiles, which could be delivered by land, sea or air, but at the same time he stepped up counterinsurgency operations to combat supposedly communist-inspired "wars of national liberation." While willing to intervene militarily, Kennedy also hoped that non-military programs such as the Peace Corps and the Alliance for Progress could change the image of the United States into that of a benefactor to the Third World.

The Kennedy administration increased defense spending on conventional forces as well as the nuclear triad. Into the mix they added a new emphasis on elite special force units such as the Green Berets, a pet project of the new president. Helicopters, in use since the Korean War but mostly for medical evacuation, would now assume a combat role by providing air mobility into remote areas amid regional conflicts.

During his abortive 1,000-day presidency Kennedy presided over the hottest days of the Cold War. Crises in Central Europe and especially in Cuba carried the palpable threat of escalating into a general nuclear war.

Inside the Kremlin Soviet leader Nikita Khrushchev faced growing pressure from right-wing militarists who had been uneasy over his denunciation of Stalin's legacy in 1956 as well as his episodic advocacy of "peaceful coexistence" with the West. Mao Zedong denounced cooperation with the Western imperialists, as an open breach developed between the two communist giants.

Khrushchev responded to the pressure from communist hardliners by drawing the line in Berlin, where the access enabling escape to the West by scientists and other East Germans precipitated a "brain drain" and had become a crisis for the communist regime. In August 1961, as tanks faced off in Berlin, East German workers began to assemble the Berlin Wall cutting off access to West Berlin. Erection of the edifice through the center of the former German capital ended the war scare but proved to be an enduring symbol of the oppression of the communist regime.

Having dodged the threat of war over Berlin, the Kennedy administration engaged in brinkmanship over the Cuban and Soviet effort secretly to equip the Caribbean island with intermediate-range nuclear weapons. The capability confronted the United States with a situation analogous to that facing the Soviet Union as a result of the intermediate-range missiles the United States had emplaced in Western Europe and in Turkey, a NATO member.

Fidel Castro had led a revolutionary guerrilla movement against the longtime US-backed military dictator in Cuba, Fulgencio Batista, culminating in his overthrow in 1959. Castro denounced the United States over its history of imperialism in Cuba and elsewhere, and eventually embraced communism. The Eisenhower administration responded with a CIA covert operation (Mongoose) to overthrow or assassinate the Cuban leader.

Kennedy inherited and then green-lighted an ill-conceived plan to land an invasion force in Cuba as the first step in a campaign leading to Castro's overthrow. In April 1961, however, the Bay of Pigs operation failed miserably as the invaders were quickly captured and the US role was widely exposed. The fiasco marked an embarrassing start to the Kennedy administration, which during the presidential campaign had condemned Eisenhower for the "loss" of Cuba.

As Khrushchev and Castro publicly gloated over the American defeat, US intelligence uncovered evidence that the communist leaders were covertly in the process of equipping Cuba with medium-range nuclear missiles. Kennedy rejected the JCS recommendation of immediate military strike against the sites, opting instead for a naval blockade—internationally recognized as an act of war--in order to impede ongoing Soviet resupply of the missile sites. Avoiding the term blockade, Kennedy announced the "quarantine" of Cuba on national television and put the US military on worldwide alert status.

The Cuban crisis is widely considered the closest the world has come to the brink of nuclear war, though a less well-known event emanating from a NATO military exercise (Able Archer 83) also nearly spun out of control in November 1983. By October 1962 tactical nuclear weapons were already operational in Cuba and could have been launched against the United States. During the crisis an American U-2 was shot down and the pilot killed. Castro, Mao, and Soviet hardliners did not want to back down to the Americans.

Much to Khrushchev's credit, cooler heads prevailed at the brink of nuclear war. As a result of secret diplomacy orchestrated by Attorney General Robert Kennedy and the Soviet diplomat Anatoly Dobrynin, Khrushchev agreed to remove the missiles in return for a tacit US agreement to withdraw American missiles from Turkey and cease efforts to topple Castro. Despite the US promise, the covert CIA assassination plots against Castro continued though they never succeeded.

The Cuban nuclear crisis had been averted and moreover created momentum for the first wave of détente, an easing of tensions. Sobered by the brush with nuclear war, Kennedy and Khrushchev agreed to establish a "hotline" for instant communication and signed the historic Limited Nuclear Test Ban Treaty terminating above-ground nuclear tests in 1963. Backing down in Cuba was one of the last straws for Khrushchev, however, as in 1964 the Soviet leader was toppled by hardliners led by Leonid Brezhnev.

With the exception of Cuba, US imperialism remained dominant in the Western Hemisphere. In 1964, in the massive and resource-rich country of Brazil, the United States bolstered and encouraged the Brazilian military to overthrow the government of Joao Goulart, a reform leader who tolerated the Communist Party and had refused to condemn Castro. That same year US occupation forces subdued anti-imperial riots in the Panama Canal zone. The Americans also toppled the democratic reform government of Cheddi Jagan in Guyana in deference to bolstering the reactionary regime under Forbes Burnham.

The United States preferred to conduct imperialism through covert or police operations, but Kennedy's successor Lyndon Johnson broke the more than 30-year tradition dating to Roosevelt's Good Neighbor Policy by mounting a direct-military intervention in the Dominican Republic. Washington had dominated the Caribbean nation politically and economically since the Theodore Roosevelt administration, but had become fed up with the formerly compliant dictator, President Rafael Trujillo, who had gone rogue with myriad acts of violent repression including an effort to assassinate the president of Venezuela. The United States closed its embassy, withdrew the ambassador, and the CIA provided weapons and encouragement to the Dominican military officers who assassinated Trujillo on May 30, 1961.

In 1962 Juan Bosch, a reform social democrat who had been exiled under Trujillo, won a sweeping victory in the first free elections in more than three decades. However, after only seven months in office Bosch was overthrown in a right-wing coup. When he moved to reclaim his government, the Johnson administration concluded that Bosch was too far to the left and might become another Castro. "I sure don't want to wake up . . . and find out Castro's in charge," Johnson declared.

On April 30, 1965, Johnson launched a military intervention that ultimately encompassed more than 40,000 Army and Marine forces. As he would do later with respect to Vietnam, Johnson blatantly misrepresented events in order to justify the direct US intervention. Johnson inflated Castro's influence as well as the threat to American lives, but the actual purpose was to restore right-wing, pro-US business conservatives over the proponents of social democracy. The change was ensconced through fraudulent elections in the wake of the military intervention.

Direct fighting included the use of tanks, machine guns, mortars, and rocket fire. Some 2,500-3,000 Dominicans were killed compared with 44 US deaths and 283 injuries. US forces withdrew in 1966, replaced by a US-dominated Organization of American States occupation force.

While the United States supported democracy in Japan and the countries of Western Europe, the Truman Doctrine pledge to support "free peoples" was proving to be empty rhetoric almost everywhere else. Virulent anti-communism, access to oil and other resources, and firm control of a hard sphere of influence in Latin America trumped democracy at every turn.

While the United States preferred to use its economic and political influence or covert operations to empower and secure the regimes that it wanted, it had also proven willing to go to war to combat left-wing governments. Johnson was determined to keep Kennedy's pledge that the United States would "pay any price, bear any burden" to contain communism. He was about to learn the hard way, however, that Vietnam was not the Dominican Republic.

Chapter 7
Losing at War

The identity driven penchant for war and imperialism produced unparalleled disaster for the United States on the Indochina Peninsula. The so-called Vietnam War--in actuality a broader conflict, the Second Indochina War--is generally considered the greatest disaster in American imperial and military history.

What Americans call the Vietnam War is correspondingly known in Vietnam as "the American war" to distinguish it from the preceding war with France--the First Indochina War. The United States thus foolishly inherited and over time dramatically escalated an anti-colonial war that France had already lost and in which it, too, had little chance of success. Application of basic historical knowledge should have enabled the United States to avoid becoming embroiled in a war of decolonization and national independence, but instead American arrogance, ignorance of history, the dictates of the Cold War, and the drives inherent in the nation's militarized foreign policy led to a prolonged intervention and a shattering defeat.

The Second Indochina War stemmed from the American determination to preclude communism from gaining a foothold in Southeast Asia. The "fall" of China and the Korean War reinforced this commitment, which had already been rooted in the decision to maintain a bloc of anti-communist nations centered around the postwar occupation of Japan and the US military presence in the neo-colonial Philippines. "Vietnam," in short, was a product of American imperialism and the global containment policy.

The French colony in Indochina was anchored economically by rubber plantations built through the pitiless exploitation of peasant labor. The Indochinese Union, promulgated in 1887 with a capital in Saigon, was the French colonial grouping of the future countries of Vietnam, Laos, and Cambodia. The British, Dutch and other Western powers colonized various other states in the sprawling region of Southeast Asia.

As throughout the colonized world, national independence movements emerged in opposition to the virulent racism, economic exploitation, and the denial of self-determination inherent in colonialism. By the time of the Great War, Ho Chi Minh—an adopted revolutionary name meaning "Bringer of Light" or "He Who Shines"—was the unquestioned leader of the Vietnamese national independence movement. Ho was a dedicated nationalist, but he also embraced Marxist-Leninist ideology--Ho was a communist.

The Second World War undermined European colonialism across the globe, giving rise to the postwar decolonization movement. The Nazi occupation of France in 1940 enabled Japan to seize authority over French Indochina later that same year. During World War II the United States and other allied forces collaborated with Ho's guerrilla independence organization, the Vietminh, to help defeat Japan. In August 1945 Ho quoted from the Declaration of Independence and a band played the Star-Spangled Banner as he declared the independent Democratic Republic of Vietnam. The United States could have cultivated support from Ho but instead would seek to destroy his anti-colonial liberation movement.

Humiliated by the Nazis, France sought to recapture its grandeur after the war by resurrecting its colonial empire. Ho made significant concessions in negotiations, but the French responded with racist contempt, precipitating the outbreak of the First Indochina War. Rather than recapture grandeur, the hapless French experienced even more profound humiliation as the Vietnamese rebels won a decisive victory culminating in 1954 at the Battle of Dienbienphu in northern Vietnam near the border with Laos.

Franklin Roosevelt had been highly critical of French rule in Indochina but following World War II the hegemonic Cold War discourse fueled the policy of global intervention against the "evil" of communism. Beginning in 1950 Truman committed millions of dollars and tons of military equipment including tanks, bombs, napalm, and automatic weapons in support of reactionary French colonialism.

Few if any American national security elites understood that the country that the Vietnamese feared most was neither France nor the United States but China. During its ancient history Vietnam had been occupied by China for nearly a *millennium*. Shared communist ideology could not overcome the legacies of a troubled history between these two neighboring states. The reason Ho had been willing to compromise with the French in 1946 was because, as he allegedly stated, "I prefer to smell French shit for five years, rather than Chinese shit for the rest of my life."

The Eisenhower administration viewed France's imminent defeat as a complete disaster, so much so that Secretary of state John Foster Dulles considered a recommendation to use nuclear weapons to end the Vietminh siege of the French base at Dienbienphu. The proposal was rejected, as the bomb proved impractical in the context of a revolutionary anti-colonial war.

Eschewing direct US intervention, Dulles instead maneuvered to undermine the Geneva Accords of 1954, an internationally brokered diplomatic solution entailing French withdrawal from Indochina to be followed by unifying elections in Vietnam. Knowing that the proposed elections in 1956 would produce a victory for Ho, who by this time had achieved the status as a veritable George Washington amid the long Vietnamese struggle for national independence, Dulles sabotaged the elections.

In Vietnam the rhetorical champion of the "free world" thus chose imperialism over democratic elections. Dulles, a skilled corporate attorney, forged the Southeast Asian Treaty Organization, an anti-communist NATO clone designed to provide a legal basis or intervention, but one that failed to inspire the nations of the region. The only members of SEATO actually from Southeast Asia were the US-backed military regimes of Thailand and the Philippines (the other SEATO members were the United States, France, Great Britain, Australia, New Zealand, and Pakistan).

The United States thus used its power and influence to subvert an international accord and chose instead to support creation of an independent, anti-communist state in southern Vietnam, where French and minority Catholic influence had been strongest. At this key moment, the United States made permanent what had been intended as a temporary division of Vietnam and thereby caused the Second Indochina War.

Many Vietnamese, including many Catholics, opposed Ho and communism, but the emperor, Bao Dai, was a discredited former French puppet hence there was no one remotely approaching Ho's status to anoint in an effort to unite the southern half of Vietnam. Desperate to find such a leader, the Americans settled on Ngo Dinh Diem, an enigmatic former monk at a Maryknoll seminary in New Jersey. Diem, a minority Catholic in a predominately Buddhist-Confucian culture, had been premier under Bao Dai's discredited former government. Diem lacked both leadership skills and popular support, yet in 1955 he proclaimed himself president of the independent Republic of Vietnam, or South Vietnam. Diem's authoritarian security regime used massive American financial and military assistance to repress widespread opposition to his rule in the south.

Preoccupied by a postwar famine and consolidation of communist rule in the north, Ho Chi Minh and his followers rejected the division of their country but were in no position to contest it militarily at the outset of Diem's regime. However, by the late 1950s the DRV began to exploit growing opposition to Diem's rule by infiltrating people and weapons in support of the National Liberation Front (NLF), formally created in

December 1960 to liberate the south and reunite the country. Diem called the NLF the "Vietcong," a slur for Vietnamese communists.

Kennedy inherited the growing instability in "South Vietnam," but he was actually more concerned about the Pathet Lao, the communist movement in neighboring Laos. However, an internationally brokered neutralization agreement at yet another Geneva Conference in 1962 put Laos on the back burner and returned Vietnam once again to the spotlight. Kennedy monitored the situation closely and indulged his zeal for special forces by increasing the number of "advisers" in Vietnam to some 16,000 by the time of his assassination.

In 1963 Diem and his brother, Ngo Dinh Nhu, who headed the South Vietnamese security police, were embroiled in the "Buddhist crisis." They badly handled widespread protests by Buddhist monks, who were being persecuted by the regime. The photograph and video of a monk who immolated himself in the streets of Saigon circulated worldwide. South Vietnam was faltering, prompting the Kennedy administration to decide that a straightforward military regime would prove more compliant and effective in repressing the growing revolutionary movement in the countryside.

In the weeks before his assassination in Dallas, Kennedy signed off on a military coup to replace the ineffectual Diem regime. On November 2, 1963 the Vietnamese military overthrew and assassinated Diem along with his brother, Nhu. Kennedy had not authorized the assassinations, but he had authorized the coup that led to them. Three weeks later Lyndon Johnson inherited the mess in Vietnam. He proceeded to make it worse— much worse.

Americanizing the War

Johnson proved all too eager to militarize the unstable political conflict that he inherited in South Vietnam. Nurtured under the New Deal in Texas, Johnson lacked foreign policy experience or sophistication. His military interventions, whether in Indochina or the Dominican Republic, had no other purpose than to ensure that no country would be lost to communism. He feared—with good reason--that the loss of any country to communism would empower the domestic right wing and potentially wreck his ambitions to implement the Great Society reform program.

As the South Vietnamese government lost ground, literally, as the NLF took over villages in the countryside, Johnson stepped up US involvement. In August 1964, amid his election campaign, Johnson publicly misrepresented a clash with North Vietnamese torpedo boats, which the United States had been secretly tracking in the Gulf of Tonkin. Johnson claimed the American ships had been subjected to a wanton attack as they were supposedly innocently minding their own business in international waters. The president claimed there were two torpedo attacks whereas there had been only one, which had done no damage to the destroyer, the USS *Maddox*. In actuality the *Maddox* had fired first, damaging three torpedo boats and killing four North Vietnamese sailors. There were no American casualties.

Johnson's actions were similar to Roosevelt's manipulation of the *Greer* incident in 1941 and part of a pattern of American presidents, at least since Polk, misrepresenting events in order to escalate US military involvement.

Johnson exploited the mendacious account of the innocuous naval incident to gain the proverbial "blank check" from Congress enabling him to take "all necessary measures" against North Vietnam. The Tonkin Gulf Resolution fended off right-wing charges amid the campaign that he was not doing enough to contain communism in Vietnam. Only two senators from the entire Congress voted against enabling the executive to wage a war far from American shores as he saw fit.

Over the ensuing months reprisal raids gave way to a regular campaign of bombing in North Vietnam. Tens of thousands of US troops and advisers poured in to help the inept South Vietnamese government attempt to contain the growing guerrilla movement in the countryside. Even before the United States undertook direct combat operations there were already some 125,000 US military personnel in the country.

The US troops and bases became an inviting target for the guerrillas, who mounted sapper attacks that took American casualties. Following one such attack on a US base at Pleiku in the Central Highlands in February 1965, killing eight Americans and destroying 10 aircraft, Johnson gave in to the military and civilian advisers who had been urging a bombing campaign against the North. He authorized Flaming Dart, a series of air attacks on North Vietnamese targets.

As the air war accelerated, General William Westmoreland, the Army field commander, requested ground forces to protect the air base at Danang from the growing threat of sapper attacks. In March 1965 two Marine Corp battalions landed in Vietnam, marking a new phase in the ground war. As the American forces at Westmoreland's behest began to undertake aggressive "search and destroy" operations, the Indochina war was becoming an American war.

Having just secured a full term in office with a landslide victory, Johnson was under little political pressure to Americanize the war. Close US allies—Canada, Britain, and France—warned against the bombing of the North and the deepening US military involvement in the South. But Johnson, who well remembered the attacks on Truman over the "loss of China," was determined to fend off the guerrillas while stabilizing the

South Vietnamese government. He wanted to show toughness and credibility, explaining that the public will "forgive you for anything except being weak."

While some advisers warned against deepening involvement in a ground war in Asia, others assumed the superior American firepower would prevail in a military conflict with a developing Third World country. Optimists could point to successful postwar counterinsurgency campaigns against radical Southeast Asian guerrilla movements in the Philippines and in Malaya. Moreover, in the fall of 1965 a failed coup in Indonesia fueled the rise of the Suharto military regime, which proceeded—with full US support--to massacre hundreds of thousands of people, effectively gutting the PKI, the Indonesian Communist Party.

Under the American imperial watch, military regimes that contained communism received fulsome support. It was of no concern how murderous they were nor how egregious their human rights records. Thus, Suharto's genocidal regime could and did kill a half a million of its own people with full US awareness and generous military assistance.

At the same time, the United States bolstered the repressive military regimes in Thailand and the Philippines, both of which provided crucial air base support for the US bombing campaign in Indochina. The US imperial heartland of Southeast Asia, the Philippines, had received independence in 1946 but like Thailand and many other regimes it was hardly part of the much ballyhooed "free world." Instead, the United States supported a military regime in the 1960s under Ferdinand Marcos, who declared martial law and shot, jailed and otherwise repressed would-be reformers. Marcos' wife Imelda personified a "let them eat cake" attitude, as she amassed an astonishing and later infamous collection of footwear.

Grunts on the Ground, Bombs in the Air

In November 1965 a major combat clash fueled a false sense of confidence among American war planners. After US Air Cavalry forces landed in a "hot" zone in the Ia Drang valley in southern Vietnam near the Cambodian border, they encountered not merely guerrillas but well-schooled and -equipped North Vietnamese Army regular units. A major fight ensued and, as was typical of the war, superior and rapidly mobilized US firepower turned the battle in the Americans' favor.

Although the US forces effectively deployed helicopter mobility, heavy artillery, and B-52 bombers to win the battle, more than 300 Americans died. More than 3,000 North Vietnamese soldiers died before the remainder escaped into neutral Cambodia. The lesson the Americans took was that the enemy could not sustain a 10-1 ratio of deaths on the battlefield, but in fact the lesson the North Vietnamese took was that despite the formidable American firepower and rapid helicopter mobility they could bloody the invaders and live to fight another day, albeit with heavy losses. They could win—just as the Americans had won their own Revolutionary War—merely by refusing to give up the fight. The Americans, they correctly surmised, eventually would grow weary of growing numbers of dead on an inconclusive and faraway battlefield.

Nothing better illustrated the illusion that superior weaponry alone could determine the outcome of the war than the failed American bombing campaign. Before the war was over the United States would unload more tonnage of bombs on Indochina than that deployed by *all belligerents in all theaters of World War II*. Despite the excess, the bombing failed to impede the guerrillas much less win the war.

Rolling Thunder, the US bombing campaign of 1965 to 1968, sought to display American credibility through graduated escalation in order to convince the North Vietnamese they would suffer greatly and could not prevail against the superior US firepower. Under the dubious premise of stabilizing the unsettled political situation in the south by bombing the north, the United States strove to damage North Vietnamese factories, industrial sites, and transportation arteries to demonstrate US resolve to cut off or severely limit supplies flowing to the guerrillas.

Despite the bombing, the southern guerrillas received an unceasing flow of people and supplies from the North down the Ho Chi Minh Trail. Far from a single path, the HCMT was a series of interconnected roads and paths, some going back for centuries and comprising thousands of miles through Vietnam as well as neighboring Laos and Cambodia. Despite the terror of the B-52 bombing raids, tens of thousands of Vietnamese took to the trail by hiking, on bicycles loaded down with supplies, and in some places through motorized transport. The Vietnamese proved adept at sounding air-raid warnings and hunkering down, as well as quickly rebuilding roads and bridges in the wake of bomb attacks.

Rolling Thunder failed utterly both in the unrealistic quest to dissuade the North Vietnamese to quit the war and in the effort to impede resupply down the HCMT. An Air Force study after war concluded that even had the bombing been more intensive from the outset, as some military advisers had recommended, it would not have worked. Bombing could not solve the political conflict in Vietnam. Some US strategists, include the longtime Defense Secretary Robert McNamara, connected the dots and concluded that the bombing campaign—of which he had been the architect—in fact would fail. He quietly resigned and years later declared, "We were wrong, we were terribly wrong."

In addition to the punishing bombing the United States engaged in a campaign of chemical warfare in Operation Ranch Hand (1962-71). The ecocide was designed to strip the guerrillas of their jungle cover by defoliating the countryside. Using diverse chemical cocktails such as Agent Orange, which contained the cancer-causing compound dioxin, the United States defoliated millions of acres. The deadly chemical war would poison the Vietnamese people as well as American and allied veterans and their children for generations.

The heedless defoliation campaign did not work, either, as the guerrillas moved to new locations and moreover tunneled underground to escape the bombing, the defoliation, as well as the search and destroy patrols. From their underground redoubts the guerrillas would emerge at night to plant mines or carry out sabotage and hit and run operations. By day snipers plagued the US combat "grunts" dispatched on foot patrols into areas unknown to them but familiar to all the locals.

Nineteen and 20-year-old American soldiers were thus assigned the role of guinea pigs, sent into dense rainforests to be attacked in order to better identify the location of the enemy to call in bombing and artillery. The Vietnamese responded to the threat of the superior US firepower by "hugging" the Americans, getting as close to them as possible in firefights to complicate the US effort to shell and bomb them into submission without hitting their own troops, which happened often enough.

As in a war in Iraq years later, the United States received little support and assistance from its allies despite the "Many Flags" program. Those who did support the American war did so for mercenary reasons, as the United States paid out millions to the dictatorial military regimes of South Korea, the Philippines and Thailand. Australia and New Zealand sent token forces whereas SEATO member Pakistan refused a US request to send troops.

The Johnson administration insisted that "pacification" was being achieved through a "war of attrition" and offered as evidence regular reports of inflated body counts of the enemy dead. The United States was in fact killing a lot of Vietnamese--civilians as well as guerrillas--but both the NLF and its North Vietnamese sponsors proved to be a highly resilient foe with an unshakeable determination to prevail in the war of "national liberation."

The military dictatorship in Saigon remained incapable of winning the "hearts and minds" of the Vietnamese public. Like South Vietnam as a whole, the generals were dependent on the Americans for their sustenance and otherwise lacked legitimacy. South Vietnam was essentially a US-created military regime falsely depicted as a viable government.

Well before McNamara lost faith, a handful of advisors including diplomat George Ball had opposed Johnson's escalation of the Indochina war. "Once you are on the tiger's back you can't decide when to get off," Ball had presciently advised. Several senators expressed private reservations but Johnson encountered formidable public opposition when Senate Foreign Relations Committee Chairman J. William Fulbright (D-AR) called hearings on the war. In 1966 Army General James Gavin as well as the architect of the containment policy, George Kennan, both offered powerful testimony raising doubts about the war and the prospects of success, noting especially the weakness of the regime in Saigon.

By 1967 the United States was already divided between "hawks and doves" on the issue of Vietnam. Church leaders of many faiths, not just Unitarians and Quakers but Jews, Catholics and Protestants as well, nurtured antiwar dissent. Polls showed growing numbers of Americans thought the war was a mistake yet also revealed that most people did not simply want to get out and let the country "fall" to communism.

Johnson contained dissent by regularly rolling out claims of high enemy body counts along with optimistic projections from Westmoreland and others. American military forces continued to wage aggressive search and destroy operations in hopes of subduing the guerrillas.

In January 1967 the United States launched Cedar Falls, the largest ground operation in the war conducted in the "Iron Triangle," an area northwest of Saigon with a heavy concentration of "Viet Cong." The operation collapsed tunnels, razed villages, and defoliated the countryside, which could then be dubbed a free-fire zone meaning that people attempting to return to their homes, farms or ancestral burial grounds would be considered "VC" and killed on sight. The mass destruction, typical of the American war in Vietnam, alienated the peasantry rather than winning over their "hearts and minds."

Later in 1967 the Americans waged a fierce fight over Dak To in the Central Highlands. The United States suffered hundreds of casualties, including 42 dead from a "friendly fire" bombing mistake. The US and South Vietnamese forces continued to bloody the NLF, which continued to escape into neighboring Cambodia to fight another day.

The North Vietnamese government, now dominated by the hardliner Le Duan, as Ho had been swept aside, was willing to sacrifice masses of lives to win the war. North Vietnamese strategists lured the Americans into the Central Highlands and had them convinced that they were poised to fight a conventional, Dienbienphu-style battle at the Khe Sanh Marine base near the Laotian border. The United States responded with a massive bombing campaign ("Niagara") and troop movements before realizing that Khe Sanh was a diversion.

At the end of January in 1968 the resistance sprang the biggest surprise attack of the war, the Tet Offensive, a massive uprising in cities and towns throughout South Vietnam. Assaulting 36 of the 44 provincial capitals,

"The enemy struck hard and with superb attention to organization, supply and secrecy," a State Department diplomat acknowledged.

Caught by surprise, the Americans had to defend targets previously assumed secure, including Tan Son Nhut Airbase and even the US Embassy compound in Saigon. Amid the chaos a South Vietnamese general summarily executed a Viet Cong suspect on the streets of Saigon, an event captured on film and providing another enduring image of the Vietnam War.

The Tet Offensive unleashed some of the most intense fighting of the war, notably the prolonged battle to recapture Hue, the imperial capital. The month-long battle culminated at the Citadel surrounding the ancient imperial palace. By the time the city had been recaptured, it was virtually destroyed. Thousands had been killed by the American shelling and bombing and in executions carried out by the communist forces against those deemed collaborators with the Saigon regime.

The Battle of Hue typified the Tet Offensive. The resistance forces failed to keep the cities and towns they had briefly occupied and suffered massive losses in the process. While the United States and the Army of the Republic of Vietnam (ARVN) allies rooted out the guerrillas, much of South Vietnam was left in ruins. As an army officer noted after the battle of Ben Tre, "We had to destroy the town to save it."

The Tet Offensive, which Hanoi later admitted had been ill-conceived and overly ambitious, failed in its ultimate purpose of unleashing a nationwide uprising toppling the Saigon regime. Yet the South Vietnam that survived Tet was reduced to a US-propelled military dictatorship grafted upon a ruined landscape filled with refugees from destroyed homes, villages and cities. The economy, including a thriving black market in drugs and prostitutes, was dependent on the American presence.

Ironically, even though the United States prevailed in the fighting, the Tet Offensive proved a political victory for the resistance and a defeat for the United States. Tet belied the Johnson administration's mendacious assurances over the course of the previous two years that pacification was working and that the communist forces were on the verge of defeat. The stunning uprising showed that the enemy was not close to being "pacified."

Westmoreland requested more than 200,000 additional troops, an escalation that incited a growing antiwar movement in the United States. Bowing to the advice of a group of elder statesmen, the "Wise Men," Johnson rejected escalation, called for negotiations backed by a bombing halt, and announced that he would not run for reelection. Westmoreland was recalled and replaced by General Creighton Abrams.

Johnson's presidency and Great Society reform agenda had been destroyed by the military intervention in Indochina. As in the world wars and the continuous Cold War, imperialism and war had shattered domestic reform efforts.

The Antiwar Movement

The disastrous Indochina intervention did, albeit relatively briefly, call into question the postwar consensus behind the global containment policy. The process began before the Tet Offensive but the bloody uprising set off a full-blown antiwar movement on the home front. Many Americans began to question the very essence of the American foreign policy of global intervention.

Inspired by the burgeoning civil rights and anti-poverty movements, campus protests began to link domestic economic and racial injustice with the faraway war against Asian peasants that US soldiers called "gooks." Students for a Democratic Society (SDS) opposed racism and the war, as a "New Left" emerged on college campuses and in coffee houses across the country.

Student opposition to the war was more than philosophical. As the Johnson administration Americanized the war, conscription compelled millions of young men to face the prospect of fighting and dying in Vietnam. The cause was so uninspiring that more than half of them took steps to avoid the war by securing college deferments, exemptions, joining the Coast Guard or the National Guard, feigning illness or medical condition, or escaping to Canada, Sweden or another country amenable to American draft evasion. Future American presidents Bill Clinton, George W. Bush and Donald Trump all took steps to avoid the draft, which made them typical rather than exceptional.

As a result of successful draft avoidance by the white middle and upper classes, African Americans and Hispanics were over-represented in the early years of the war. In 1965, African Americans constituted 31 percent of US forces in Vietnam though they were only 12 percent of the US population. Publicity over the issue in the era of racial unrest brought changes, spurring a reduction in African American participation and casualty rates, which ended up being roughly representative of the population by the end of the war.

Poorer and working-class Americans continued to be overrepresented as the upper and middle classes who benefitted from greater access to college and other means successfully avoided the draft. The unpopularity and patent unfairness of the draft propelled an end to conscription, very likely permanently, in American history. In 1969 a draft lottery attempted to restore pure luck of the draw to make the system fairer but by then direct US participation began to wind down. In 1973 the United States terminated conscription in deference to an all-volunteer army. Over the ensuing years, the new system perpetuated an old result as the upper and middle classes continued to avoid military service, leaving military service in the hands primarily of more economically challenged Americans, substantial numbers of them Black and Hispanic.

Antiwar demonstrations took place throughout the Vietnam War, but they exploded after the Tet Offensive and brought everyday life in cities and college towns to a standstill. In 1968 students rioted and occupied buildings at New York's Columbia University, a tactic that spread to other campuses. In August the Democratic National Convention in Chicago devolved into anarchy, as antiwar protesters flocked to the city whose Democratic Mayor Richard Daley responded by unleashing a baton-wielding "police riot" on peaceful demonstrators and innocent bystanders.

The presidential election of Republican Richard M. Nixon heightened the divisions in the country. Nixon condemned campus protesters as well as racial unrest, as he campaigned on a "law and order" theme.

After his narrow election victory Nixon enjoyed a brief "honeymoon" from war protesters but then in October 1969 some 500,00 attended the "Moratorium" in Washington demanding a prompt end to the war. The president declared he was ignoring the demonstration in deference to watching a college football game. In a televised speech he called on the "great silent majority" of Americans to back him up and silence the protesters.

Peaceful protest gave way to rage-filled demonstrations when Nixon announced at the end of April 1970 an "incursion" into Cambodia, which was being sucked into the war by Vietnamese violations of its territory and US bombing. Cambodian President Norodom Sihanouk had long condemned US intervention in Indochina, but he was overthrown in a military coup, propelling Cambodia into a war that would lead to destruction and genocide.

On May 4, 1970, the day after the burning of the ROTC building at Kent State University in northeastern Ohio, the Ohio National Guard inexplicably sprayed gunfire into a crowd of angry but peaceful protesters, killing four students--one an ROTC member making his way to class. At the University of Wisconsin (UW) students occupying campus buildings were beaten by police. In August a bomb exploded in the UW Army Math Research Center, killing one man. In April 1971 a massive antiwar march descended on Washington.

The continuing campus protests angered Nixon, who responded with illegal spying and surveillance. Nixon's self-destructive Watergate scandal was rooted in his contempt for civil rights and antiwar protesters, among other entrants into his meticulously maintained "enemies list."

The racist and right-wing longtime FBI Director J. Edgar Hoover launched the COINTELPRO program entailing widespread infiltration, harassment and illegal spying on antiwar as well as civil rights groups. Once again, as in previous American conflicts dating to the 1790s, war abroad eroded civil liberties on the home front.

Nixon's Failed Strategy

During the presidential campaign Nixon pledged to withdraw US troops and to "Vietnamize" the war, but the quest for "peace with honor" meant the United States would not get out and accept defeat—at least not until 1973. Heavy bombing thus continued and about half the total US casualties occurred under Nixon.

Nixon's "plan" to end the war "with honor" encompassed troop withdrawals and better equipment and training of the South Vietnamese armed forces ("Vietnamization"). The self-described "madman" component to Nixon's strategy entailed intensified bombing and other aggressive actions designed to make the North Vietnamese fear that Nixon might do anything to prevail if they failed to facilitate "peace with honor."

Nixon and his foreign policy confidante, the Harvard academic Henry A. Kissinger, sought to increase pressure on China and the USSR to compel Hanoi to come to terms that the Americans could accept. With the Soviets and the Chinese at each other's throats—they engaged in a border war in 1969--the US leaders had finally come to understand and attempt to exploit the profound divisions within the "communist world."

"Nixinger" sought to capitalize on the Soviet-Chinese hostilities by engaging in "triangular diplomacy," playing the communist giants off against one another by offering each incentive for closer cooperation with the United States. Amid great fanfare, Nixon, the lifelong perfervid anti-communist, visited both Beijing and Moscow as he and Kissinger carried out the new policy of détente, including securing arms control accords with the USSR and moving toward formal diplomatic recognition of "Red China."

The flaw in the strategy as far as Vietnam was concerned was the notion that the two communist giants could compel the communist leaders in Hanoi to come to terms that would include the preservation of an independent "South Vietnam." The logic behind triangular diplomacy—that the communist world was not united—should have led to the logical conclusion that neither Mao nor the Kremlin, should they even prove willing, could force Le Duan and the Hanoi communists to abandon their war of national liberation.

The Soviets had their own reasons to pursue détente but warming relations with the Americans would not preclude them from continuing to deliver war materiel including surface-to-air missiles, which shot down scores of American B-52 and other aircraft. Beginning in 1965 China had sent more than 300,000 troops and advisers across its border into North Vietnam, ensuring that any US direct invasion of the north would lead again, as in Korea, to war with the most populous and fanatical communist regime in the world.

Vietnamization, heavy bombing, "madman" theories, escalation into Laos and Cambodia, and encouraging words from Moscow and Beijing failed to cohere into a viable strategy that could change the realities on the ground. Under Nixon the war was still being lost and South Vietnam still could not survive without the United States propping it up.

Intense fighting and massive death and destruction continued throughout Nixon's first term to no real purpose. Nothing better symbolized the senselessness of the war than the May 1969 fight for Dong Ap Bia, or "Hamburger Hill" as it was fittingly if grotesquely named, which the Army's 101st Airborne finally took in a blood-drenched fight. After fighting and dying their way to the top of the mountain, the US forces found a few Vietnamese cadres had bound themselves to trees symbolizing their intention to die for the cause. The 101st summarily abandoned the hill after taking it, with the Army explaining that it actually had no strategic value. For the United States Ap Bia had just been a place where the enemy could be engaged and killed.

For many Americans the Hamburger Hill battle underscored the senselessness of the ongoing conflict, which also produced increasing evidence of US atrocities. The infamous My Lai massacre of March 16, 1968 came to light, revealing that Army Lieutenant William Calley, who was charged with war crimes but later condemned only to three years of house arrest by Nixon, led a rage-filled assault in which some 500 mostly women, children and elderly villagers were slaughtered. The incident was far from isolated as other individuals and units such as the Army's Tiger Force squad perpetrated rape, mass murder and mutilation. In 1968 the CIA launched the secret Phoenix program in which tens of thousands of Vietnamese villagers were assassinated some on mere suspicion of being rebels.

Nixon impeded inquiries into US atrocities and stepped up his own belligerence as his "plan" failed to deliver the desired results. Indulging the "madman" component of his strategy, Nixon in the spring of 1972 responded to a North Vietnamese offensive with unprecedented firepower, explaining as he unleashed Operation Linebacker that he intended to "bomb those bastards like they've never been bombed before . . . We won't aim for civilians but if a few bombs slop over, that's just too bad." He also took the unprecedented escalatory step of mining Haiphong Harbor where Soviet shipments were delivered.

In October 1972, a month before Nixon's reelection, Kissinger, who had entered into secret peace talks with North Vietnam's Le Duc Tho, announced "peace is at hand." However, South Vietnamese President Nguyen Van Thieu balked at the prospect of US withdrawal absent North Vietnamese recognition of his regime. North Vietnam held the upper hand, as its troops occupied substantial areas of South Vietnam, especially up and down the borders with Cambodia and Laos. Nixon blamed North Vietnam rather than Thieu for the breakdown of the October agreement and unleashed Linebacker II, the most punishing B-52 bombing of the war, including hitting a hospital and other civilian targets in Hanoi, among other heavily bombed North Vietnamese cities.

At last, in January 1973, the signing of the Paris Treaty marked an agreement on US withdrawal. Thieu remained the titular leader of what was left of South Vietnam, but the United States had abandoned his dreamlike demand that the North Vietnamese troops withdraw from the considerable portions of the South that they occupied.

Whether Nixon and Kissinger had merely settled for a "decent interval" between US withdrawal and the inevitable fall of South Vietnam, or intended to re-intervene if necessary, will never be known, as Nixon was forced to resign as president in August 1974 over a series of illegal and impeachable offenses comprising the Watergate scandal.

With the Americans and Nixon gone and the North Vietnamese troops ensconced in the South, the Thieu regime's days were numbered. Not even the North Vietnamese, however, expected their 1975 offensive to proceed seamlessly, but so it did as the communist forces rolled through the southern cities and into Saigon--which today is known as Ho Chi Minh City.

Consequences of the War

Some 2.7 million American men (and some 11,000 women, mostly military nurses) served in Vietnam. More than 58,000 Americans died, some 46,000 of them killed in action or from battle wounds and the rest from accidents (more than 9,000), disease, and other causes. More than 300,000 were wounded and 75,000 left physically disabled, though many of these men would have died in previous wars absent their rapid evacuation by helicopter.

The mental toll of an unpopular, terror-filled war in a phantasmagorical setting was extremely high but Americans were slow to recognize and offer treatment for Post-Traumatic Stress Disorder (PTSD). The psychological disorder was not officially designated by the American Psychiatric Association until 1980. While actual numbers are disputed, and many veterans readjusted well to society, it is clear that Vietnam veterans exceeded national averages in alcoholism, drug abuse, suicide, spouse abuse, violent crime, incarceration, and many other categories relating to the trauma inflicted upon them by the war.

Preoccupied with the impact that "Vietnam" had exacted upon the United States, Americans generally paid far less attention to the impact of the nation's unbridled militarism on Indochina. Vietnam suffered some three million dead, 14 million wounded and hundreds of thousands of others missing. Tens of thousands more would die or be maimed in ensuing years from unexploded ordinance left behind by the indiscriminate American militarism. The toxic and indiscriminate herbicidal warfare left millions of acres destroyed and hundreds of thousands of victims of cancer and birth defects. With Vietnam's infrastructure devastated, millions of people were left homeless, unemployed and destitute. Hundreds of thousands of "boat people" fled the country. Many died at sea, fell victim to piracy, or encountered rejection if they made it into foreign ports. Hundreds of thousands of South Vietnamese immigrated to the United States.

Bitter in defeat, the United States in sharp contrast to its approach to Germany and Japan after World War II isolated Vietnam and subjected the war-ravaged country to a punitive array of economic sanctions. Vietnam allied closely with the Soviet Union, which failed however to inspire the Vietnamese people who created a new slang word for Russians which roughly translated as, "Americans without money."

Polls showed that a majority of Americans long subscribed to a baseless conspiracy theory—that Vietnam was holding US soldiers as captive years after the war ended. Tawdry but popular Hollywood films such as the "Rambo" series and "Missing in Action" glorified missions returning to Vietnam to free the fictional hostages. Various groups raised funds and paid their executives high salaries promoting the mythology. In actuality, the Vietnam War featured by far the best accounting of the fate of soldiers missing in action than any other war to that time in American history. Despite myriad false sightings and fake videos, no evidence of a single American being held after the war's end ever materialized.

Another myth with virtually no basis in fact held that antiwar protesters spat upon US soldiers when they returned home. The popular myth neatly obscured that thousands of US military personnel took part in the antiwar movement, forming the influential group Vietnam Veterans Against the War. While the image of the spat upon veteran became ensconced in national mythology, celebrity antiwar protesters notably the actor Jane

Fonda were condemned for their activism and in her case spat upon at a book signing in 2005.

Hostile discourse and representation cast aspersions on the media and antiwar protesters while perpetuating hatred of the Vietnamese, thereby bolstering the economic embargo. Not until 1995 did the United States normalize relations with Vietnam and open a US embassy in Hanoi. By the twenty-first century the United States and Vietnam were increasingly allied in containing Chinese aggressiveness in the South China Sea.

The American war heavily victimized Cambodia and Laos, leaving the small and desperately poor Indochinese nations devastated. In Laos the CIA waged a long covert war against the Pathet Lao and the United States bombed relentlessly—so relentlessly that the tiny land-locked nation of Laos is, absurdly, the most heavily bombed country per capita in human history. In Laos the United States allied with an ethnic minority, the Hmong, and then summarily abandoned them to the mercies of the Pathet Lao.

The greatest horror, an outright genocide, descended on Cambodia, which had been stable under Sihanouk, whom the Americans helped drive out and replace with a military regime in 1970 because he sharply opposed US intervention. The military junta did not last and ultimately was overthrown by fanatical Maoists, the Khmer Rouge, who perpetrated the genocide after taking power in 1975. Over the next four years the fanatics deurbanized the society and killed some 1.7 million people, hundreds of thousands through executions but most by disease and famine.

The Third Indochina War erupted in 1978 when Vietnam invaded Cambodia, which had targeted ethnic Vietnamese, among other victims. China, allied with Cambodia, responded by invading northern Vietnam where they met with stiff resistance and quickly pulled out. The Third Indochina War underscored the misperceptions that took Americans into the conflict in the first place, as it ended with four communist regimes fighting amongst each other, as opposed to the American Cold War vision of a monolithic communist movement marching in lockstep to take over the world.

The Americans' contempt for the Vietnamese and Soviets was such that in the UN the United States supported Chinese military assistance to the Khmer Rouge. The United States even voted in favor of recognizing the genocidal regime as the legitimate government of Cambodia. In 1991 accords in Paris finally brought an end to the conflict, but decades later Cambodia remained desperately poor and shattered by the Indochina wars.

Chapter 8
Reviving Imperialism and War

A disaster of immense proportions, "Vietnam" nonetheless did not usher in a fundamental rethinking nor meaningful change in American foreign policy. Despite the debacle, it took relatively little time to revivify the identity-driven American imperial mission in world affairs--thus underscoring how deeply ensconced it was and remains.

In the immediate aftermath of the Indochina wars, Watergate, and the revelations of illegal CIA activities, President Jimmy Carter pledged to transform US foreign policy and make human rights the centerpiece of his diplomacy. Following his election in 1976, Carter encountered entrenched opposition and had the bad timing of being president when the blowback set in from the long history of US imperialism in the Middle East (next chapter). The powerful wave of blowback brought an economy-stagnating energy crisis as well as the wrenching hostage crisis with Iran in 1979.

Carter's successor, Republican Ronald Reagan, elected by a landslide in 1980, revivified imperialism and war at the center of US foreign policy. Thus, by the 1980s any "lessons" about the excesses and contradictions of US imperialism arising out of the Indochina War had been shelved. Reagan declared that Vietnam intervention had been a "noble cause" that had been lost only because of a lack of will owing to the proverbial stab in the back of the antiwar movement and the "liberal media." While the former Hollywood actor skillfully made his case with the public, millions of Americans flocked to theaters to watch "Rambo: First Blood Part II" (1985), the saga of a lone, neglected Vietnam veteran who now received a secret mission to return to Indochina. "Do we get to win this time?" Rambo queried, thus affirming the Reagan stab in the back exculpation for the American defeat in Vietnam.

Despite a series of foreign policy fiascos under Reagan, including support for murderous regimes, a disastrous intervention in Lebanon, and the bone-headed Iran-contra scandal, Reagan was destined to be remembered as a "great" president. An inveterate anti-communist, Reagan had drawn a hard line on the Soviet Union and thus received credit in the minds of many for its collapse shortly after he left office.

The disintegration of the Soviet empire flowed from internal contradictions, exacerbated to be sure by the effort to keep pace with

American defense spending and foreign intervention, but in the popular imagination, Reagan and the United States had "won" the Cold War. In 1991, the same year the USSR fell apart, the United States crushed Iraq in the Persian Gulf War, an unambiguous military victory that set into motion, however, generations of fruitless US intervention in that horrifically besieged nation.

In the wake of the end of the Cold War and the pummeling of Iraq, an academic pundit declared that the "end of history" had arrived, as American-led liberal capitalism was now the only viable model for human progress worldwide. As Reagan had avowed, America was back as the proverbial "shining city on a hill" that all the world should emulate. The economy, fueled by new oil supplies and the Silicon Valley microchip revolution, took off in the 1990s, affirming in the minds of many US global preeminence.

Under the "Washington consensus," the United States demanded free trade, privatization, and government deregulation and austerity programs as a condition of assistance from the Washington-based global financial institutions. Under this "globalization" regime, multi-national corporations and financial elites all over the world profited while impoverished people languished as health, education and social welfare declined. Even after massive economic collapses such as the Asian financial crisis of 1997-98 and the Great Recession of 2007-09, the United States remained wedded to the classical economic model, alternately punishing and rewarding other countries in all regions for their compliance or resistance.

Other than promoting the Washington consensus, American foreign policy lacked definition following the sudden end of the Cold War—that is until September 11, 2001. The resulting Global War on Terror (GWOT) mirrored the Cold War as well as earlier enduring frameworks such as Manifest Destiny and making the world "safe for democracy." All flowed from the national identity of American exceptionalism and the attendant right to lead the supposedly free world.

During the GWOT, as in the Cold War, the United States engaged in imperialism and war to enforce its neo-liberal capitalist economic system and to support undemocratic, militarized, and often outright fascistic regimes.

Asian Imperialism

In East Asia the United States successfully shepherded occupied Japan into its postwar role as a demilitarized economic powerhouse. Ironically, by the 1970s Japan was outperforming the United States in key industries notably automobiles and electronics, contributing to the US economic struggles in the 1970s.

Actual American support for democracy and the rule of law in Japan, as in Western Europe, can be accounted as the primary success stories of postwar US foreign policy. The American presence in East Asia also anchored a tenuous balance of power in the region, keeping in check potentially explosive enmities that remained palpable between the former wartime belligerents Japan, China, and Korea. Diplomatic engagement, backed by a defensive military presence, thus can in certain cases prove effective.

Managing relations with China became a crucially important element of East Asian diplomacy. In the midst of the effort to bomb their way out of Vietnam, devastating Cambodia and Laos in the process, Nixon and Kissinger forged the long overdue new relationship with "Red China." While recognizing "one China" and opening up trade and cultural relations with Beijing, the United States nonetheless continued to support Taiwan, which operated under martial law until the late 1980s. Like South Korea, Taiwan thus did not transition to democracy until the late 1980s.

Elsewhere in Asia and Southeast Asia US imperialism succored brutally repressive military regimes, some which put into effect with full American support policies that were clearly genocidal. Nixon's rapid political descent in the Watergate crimes, culminating in resignation in August 1974, left Kissinger at helm of US foreign policy under the caretaker President Gerald R. Ford. Kissinger was a much ballyhooed but completely amoral "statesman" who ensured that US imperialism and indifference to democracy and human rights prevailed throughout the Nixon-Ford years—not only in Asia but worldwide.

A Jewish refugee from Nazi Germany, Kissinger became a Harvard academic and a Eurocentric "realist" who exalted the "national interest," the utility of nuclear weapons, and great power diplomacy. Global issues such as decolonization, economic and racial inequality and human rights were of little interest to him. With the approval of the like-minded Nixon and the acquiescent Ford, Kissinger enabled and rewarded a series of right-wing if not outright fascist "allies" as they carried out horrendous acts of violent oppression.

The South Asian nation of Pakistan played an essential role as intermediary in the breakthrough with China, which prompted Nixon and Kissinger to "tilt" toward the Pakistani military regime at the expense of its rival India--the largest functioning democracy in the world. While Pakistan acted as the go-between in Kissinger's secret visit to China in 1971, the militarists in Islamabad carried out a genocidal campaign killing as many as 800,000 people in East Pakistan. India intervened, halted the carnage, crushed Pakistan in war, and the new nation of Bangladesh replaced East Pakistan in March 1971.

The United States had not intervened directly, yet the tilt to Pakistan had enabled a genocidal assault of which it was fully aware. Nixon and Kissinger could have made clear to their military client in Islamabad that they would not fund and support Pakistan's indiscriminately violent and imperial policy, but they chose not to do so. "The role of Nixon and Kissinger in this tragedy was, at a minimum, shameful," political scientist Salim Mansur notes, as the global superpower had green-lighted "a campaign of terror and mass murder against an unarmed civilian population."

Defeat in Indochina heightened the American determination to maintain US-allied regimes, no matter what their character, across Southeast Asia. The United States backed military governments in Thailand and the Philippines. Thailand remains a military regime today whereas the Philippines democratized in the late 1980s but has maintained a repressive security state that became increasingly draconian after the inauguration of President Rodrigo Duterte in 2016.

From the mid-1960s to 1998 the United States bolstered the murderous Suharto regime in Indonesia. After the Johnson administration had cheered on the bloodbath following the 1965 overthrow of President Sukarno, in which hundreds of thousands of leftists, reformers and professionals were slaughtered, the United States lavished military assistance on General Suharto's crony capitalist regime, which fully subscribed to the Washington consensus.

In 1974 Indonesia's militarists sought to annex East Timor after the overthrow of the military dictatorship in Lisbon spurred the dissolution of the Portuguese empire, of which East Timor had been a part. Differences in history, language, religion and culture separated East and West Timor, the latter of which had long been absorbed into the Indonesian nation. Kissinger explicitly provided a US stamp of approval to Suharto's invasion of East Timor, which began not coincidentally the day after President Ford departed from a state visit to Jakarta in December 1975.

The ensuing indiscriminate killing by Indonesian forces of the independence-seeking Fretilin guerrillas as well as non-combatant civilians, who also endured famine, totaled as many as 200,000 people—or about a third of the entire population of East Timor. The brutal repression coincided with billions of dollars in US military assistance to Indonesia, both of which continued for more than a generation until the overthrow of Suharto in 1998. The next year East Timor finally received independence.

Absent the American green light from Ford and Kissinger and the massive shipment of arms and military assistance to Suharto's regime, as geographer Joseph Nevins points out, "It is highly doubtful that the invasion would have taken place or that the occupation would have endured to the depth, extent, and duration that it did." As in the tilt to Pakistan, US policy had been characterized by support for imperialism and mass murder.

Elsewhere in the Asia-Pacific region the United States shored up its imperial presence with the major military bases in Hawaii, Okinawa, Thailand, and the Philippines, as well as through its Pacific island colonies. Militarized colonial outposts include Guam, the Federated States of Micronesia, and the Republic of the Marshall Islands. Variously organized as "freely associated" or "unincorporated territories," the hundreds of thousands of Pacific islanders do not enjoy the full rights of US citizenship. They receive some US benefits but are under the ultimate authority of the President and Congress--for which they cannot vote. The Pacific islands, in sum, are occupied militarized outposts and colonized territories.

Choosing Murderous Militarism over Democracy in Latin America

In no region was the imperial continuity of the United States more evident than in the "backyard" of Latin America. The United States continued as it had since 1960 to seethe over the defiance of the openly communist and Soviet-allied Castro regime in Cuba. Washington maintained a tight economic embargo over Cuba, which suffered from the isolation but nonetheless instituted antipoverty, literacy and health care reforms superior to those of other nations in the hemisphere—including the United States. Castro sat at the head of an authoritarian government, but the political repression on the island, while real, paled in comparison with that of many US allies.

Castro continued to cast a long shadow, however, as his presence served as the motivation and justification for myriad US imperial interventions in the region. Though overshadowed by the disastrous escalation in Vietnam, Johnson had embraced Brazilian militarists over democracy and had intervened in Panama in 1964 and invaded the Dominican Republic in 1965, all to ensure that no new leftists came to power in the hemisphere.

In 1970 the election in Chile of Salvador Allende, a physician and socialist reformer who had been active in the Pacific nation's parliamentary democracy since the 1930s, was intolerable to the imperial superpower to the north. Reelected in 1972 amid great fanfare over the dramatic breakthroughs of "triangular diplomacy" with Russia and China, Nixon and Kissinger were free to encourage and fund a blatant subversion of democracy followed by lavish support for the ensuing fascistic regime in Chile.

The United States strove to make the Chilean economy "scream" while continuing however to pump millions into the right-wing military. In 1970 the CIA colluded in the assassination of General René Schneider who had vowed to uphold the well-established democratic tradition in Chile in the wake of Allende's election. Allende pursued socialist style reform but did so constitutionally, as he refused to rule with an iron fist, thus leaving him vulnerable to the coup that the United States, Brazil and other right-wing Latin American states encouraged.

As Kissinger later acknowledged the United States "created the conditions as great as possible" for a coup while ensuring as he put it at the time that, "Our hand doesn't show." On September 11, 1973 the Chilean military unleashed tanks and warplanes on the national palace in Santiago. Inside, Allende delivered a final radio address and committed suicide. The Chilean military proceeded to round up, torture and murder of some 3,500 people, including three US citizens. As the coup unfolded the United States immediately declared its "desire to cooperate with the military junta," which it promptly and cynically recognized as the legitimate government of Chile.

General Augusto Pinochet orchestrated a "Caravan of Death," systematically tracking down and "disappearing" alleged leftists and reformers. Nixon and Kissinger continued to make clear their unstinting imperial support of murderous military repression over democracy, particularly as Chile ended Allende's effort to nationalize resources and signed on to the Washington consensus. In 1976 Kissinger assured Pinochet, "We are sympathetic with what you are trying to do here . . . We want to help." Three months later the son of a US corporate executive in Chile perpetrated a car bombing on Embassy Row in Washington, D.C. in collusion with the Chilean secret police, DINA. The bombing killed Orlando Letelier, a Chilean diplomat who condemned the military takeover and repression, as well as a US citizen riding in the car with him, Ronni Moffit. The administration authorized disinformation assuring the US public that "intelligence officials" had "virtually ruled out" the Pinochet regime's responsibility for the terror attack in the US capital.

The US backing for far-right militarism in Chile was part of a broader campaign—Operation Condor—embracing military repression throughout Latin America. Militarism, corporate capitalism, including extraction of resources such as Chilean copper, and hostility to democracy and progressive reform were the essence of US policy. In myriad countries including Argentina, Bolivia, Brazil, Paraguay and Uruguay, the United

States funded military dictators as they carried out assassination, torture and terror campaigns against reformers and left-wing political opponents.

For decades the US Army trained Latin American militarists in techniques of repression at the School of the Americas (SOA). Originally established in Panama in 1946, the SOA moved to Fort Benning, Georgia, where it remains today, though it has been innocuously renamed the "Western Hemisphere Institute for Security Cooperation." By encouraging, funding, training and supporting repressive military regimes, the United States avoided direct intervention while still pursuing its imperial economic and security policies in the hemisphere.

In Argentina as in Chile, Washington encouraged vicious military repression including thousands of people "disappeared" from 1976 to 1983 by the US-backed military regime. As in other venues throughout the world, Kissinger gave an unambiguous "green light" to the campaign against "subversion," advising only, "If there are things to be done you should do them quickly." The Argentine generals got the message, unleashing the "dirty war" against leftists, trade unions, students, teachers and the poor, killing some 30,000 people in all.

US imperialism in the smaller countries of Central America was more direct than in Argentina, Chile and the Condor states. The rise of left-wing regimes backed by Cuba was anathema to US imperialism, which for generations had pursued absolute control over Central America and the Caribbean.

Elected in 1976 in part as a backlash against the "Nixinger" amorality in foreign policy as well as in Watergate, Carter made human rights the centerpiece of his diplomatic discourse. The Georgia Democrat encountered myriad obstacles, however, and his enforcement was selective and sometimes hypocritical, as he embraced repressive military regimes in allied countries such as South Korea and most infamously and consequentially in his support for the Shah of Iran.

In Argentina the Carter administration condemned the "dirty war" and cut back on economic and political support of it. Late in his one-term presidency, however, Carter initiated direct intervention against the social and political reform movements in Central America, setting the stage for a broader campaign of intervention under Reagan.

Reagan and right-wing Republicans condemned Carter for undermining US imperial control over Latin America as reflected in the "giveaway" of the Panama Canal in a 1979 treaty. Under the long overdue treaty, the United States would turn over control of the canal to Panama in 20 years' time yet reserve the option of US military intervention if any attempt were made to close off the waterway. The treaty barely received the required two-thirds vote in the Senate. At the same time, right-wing US imperialists conveniently "discovered" and loudly trumpeted a Soviet "combat brigade" in Cuba, which in actuality was a small contingency force that had been on the island with US knowledge since 1962.

Following his election Reagan authorized a concerted imperial campaign, including US backing for an outright genocide in Guatemala. The United States had long dominated the small Central American nation in which it had ensconced militarists in the wake of the "successful" 1954 CIA coup ousting the reformer Jacobo Arbenz. The SOA-trained Guatemalan militarists took the repression to a new level, however, in "*la violencia*," which unfolded with full US support from 1978-84.

Guatemalan militarists attacked more than 600 villages, destroying more than two-thirds of those, and killed or "disappeared" more than 200,000 Guatemalans. The Guatemalan genocide targeted the left but even more so the indigenous Maya, who accounted for more than 80 percent of the victims.

The Reagan administration underwrote and encouraged the mass murder. US officials were fully informed about the atrocities being perpetrated in Guatemala. In December 1982 Reagan nonetheless met with and praised General Rios Montt as "a man of great integrity" who was "totally dedicated to democracy." In 2013 Montt was convicted in Guatemala of crimes against humanity for "masterminding the genocide."

In addition to embracing the Guatemalan genocide Reagan openly touted his commitment to driving out the left-wing government of Nicaragua and destroying the rebel movement in tiny neighboring El Salvador. He unleashed the CIA, which worked with Salvadoran military "death squads" while at the same time converting Honduras into a US-led paramilitary staging ground for attacks on the Sandinista left-wing government in Nicaragua. The Sandinistas were named for Augusto Sandino, a martyred rebel from the 1930s that the US-backed Somoza regime had assassinated in 1934 in order to stifle reform. In 1979 the Sandinistas ousted the thoroughly corrupt and decrepit Somoza government and replaced it with a socialist regime backed by Castro and the Soviet Union, but also recognized by the countries of Western Europe. In 1984 the Sandinista government prevailed in a democratic election.

Dedicated to imperial repression rather than democracy, the Reagan administration sponsored and trained Contra rebels, comprised mostly of Somoza's former national guard. Reagan called the Contras "freedom fighters," but they were in actuality murderous militarists. Human rights groups pointed out that the Contras "systematically engaged in violent abuses . . . as their principal means of waging war." The Contras killed the poor, professionals and anyone who supported the left-wing government. The CIA covertly supported the Contras and also illegally mined Nicaragua's harbors, which the International Criminal Court in the Netherlands, unrecognized by the United States, condemned in 1986.

When the US Congress cut off funding for the Contras as a result of publicity over their violent excesses, the Reagan administration resorted to a hare-brained scheme in which it covertly raised money from a bizarre range of sources—from Central American drug lords to illicit arms sales to the hated "terrorist" regime in Iran—and diverted the profits to the Contras. The Iran-contra scandal was exposed in 1985, tarnishing the Reagan administration that was also complicit in enabling the plundering of the US public in a simultaneous and far-reaching savings and loan scandal.

The Sandinistas endured as a force in Nicaraguan politics. More than 30,000 people died in the Nicaraguan conflict, most of them killed by the US-backed Contras.

The Reagan administration embraced even more murderous militarism in El Salvador, as the government gave free rein to the "death squads" that roamed the country killing indiscriminately. The killings included Catholic Archbishop Oscar Romero, assassinated while conducting mass, and four American churchwomen, raped and murdered amid their missionary work in the impoverished country. In December 1981 the US-backed Salvadoran military slaughtered the entire village of some 800 residents of El Mozote. The government death squads remained active until a 1992 agreement in Mexico City brought an end to the conflict. Most of the estimated 70,000 people killed in El Salvador, a country of only 5.3 million in total, died at the hands of the US-backed death squads.

Reagan and his Vice President and eventual successor, George H.W. Bush, launched direct US military interventions in Grenada and Panama. After radicals took over the tiny eastern Caribbean island of Grenada in a bloody coup in October 1983, Reagan green-lighted an already drawn up plan of invasion in which 8,000 US forces stormed the island and deposed the regime. The assault killed scores of people, including 18 in a misguided airstrike on a psychiatric hospital. Britain and the UN condemned the invasion but in the wake of defeat in Vietnam and a devastating attack on US Marines in Lebanon just two days earlier—from which Reagan deflected attention by authorizing the Grenada assault—most of the American public cheered the fish-in-a-barrel military operation.

In December 1989 President Bush sent 26,000 US forces into Panama to depose the dictator Manuel Noriega, a longtime CIA "asset" in the region who made the mistake of openly defying the United States while at the same time having his political opponents beaten in the streets. Hundreds of Panamanians compared with 26 Americans died in the asymmetric attack. An entire neighborhood was destroyed in the all-out assault, the largest US military operation since Vietnam. Thousands of Panamanians were arrested, including union leaders, students and professors, merely because they opposed "Operation Just Cause." Noriega spent the rest of his life in prison where he could not discuss inside information about his longtime association with the CIA, which had enabled his profiteering from cocaine trafficking in return for assistance in the Contra war and other covert activities. Most Americans approved the Panama invasion, but the Organization of American States and the UN criticized the unilateral US military assault.

The United States intervened twice to quell unrest in Haiti, in 1994 and again in 2004. Washington was mainly concerned about the "threat" of Haitian refugees and, in the second intervention, that reforms by the popularly elected leader Jean-Bertrand Aristide would go too far—for example in raising the minimum wage beyond the prevailing $3 an hour. Washington did not want Haiti to undermine the US-mandated neo-liberal economic policies under which the island was deeply indebted to US banks. After forcing out Aristide, the United States led a humanitarian intervention in 2010 in the wake of a devastating earthquake in Haiti, which remained desperately poor and mired in corruption and militancy.

The continuous US policy of resolutely opposing left-wing reform governments, whether they were elected or not, continued in the twenty-first century. The United States typically supported conservatives and reactionaries in an effort to oust leftists, who defied the Washington consensus and had gained power at various times through elections in Bolivia, Brazil, Chile, Ecuador, Nicaragua and Peru.

In addition to the ongoing effort to isolate, sanction and undermine the Castro regime, the United States backed a 2002 coup against Hugo Chavez, a Castro ally who was popularly elected and repeatedly reelected in Venezuela mainly because he pursued racial justice and provided food and health care to the impoverished masses. After Chavez died of cancer in 2013, Nicholas Maduro, his legally elected successor, became increasingly autocratic as the United States and the mostly lighter-skinned, right-wing Venezuelan opposition tried to oust him. In 2019 President Donald Trump recognized a wholly illegitimate self-proclaimed successor to Maduro, a tactic that succeeded only in making Maduro more autocratic.

Trump reversed an effort by his predecessor Barack Obama, to at long last normalize relations with Cuba, an action that pleased the vocal Cuban American right wing centered in Miami. Trump offered fulsome support for his reactionary ideological clone in Brazil, President Jair Bolsonaro, who came to power in 2018 after several years of left-leaning reform governments in the vast Latin American nation. Like Trump, Bolsonaro disputed the science of climate change and cavalierly put to the torch ever more of the disappearing Brazilian rainforest.

In the 1990s the United States negotiated a free trade agreement with Canada and Mexico, both of which often but not always sided with the United States in foreign affairs. Anxiety flared regularly with Mexico over illegal migration across the US border. In 2016 Trump pledged but failed to build a border wall after claiming absurdly that Mexico would pay for it.

Beginning in the 1970s the United States waged an ill-conceived and militarized "war" on drugs, which it lost both at home and abroad. Blaming suppliers rather than dealing constructively with the voracious US appetite for drugs of all varieties, Washington pumped billions of dollars into Plan Colombia and similar paramilitary drug wars in Latin America. Appropriating the discourse of the GWOT, these campaigns supported repressive regimes against "narco-terrorists." In reality, as in the case of Colombia, the right-wing government, not just the guerrillas, was an active player in the lucrative drug trade. When the Colombian and other paramilitaries aided by US forces did find and destroy coca fields, growers simply moved to a new location or a neighboring country, such as Peru. Drug cultivators and suppliers across the globe--from marijuana growers in the United States to poppy farmers in Afghanistan--adopted these same tactics, which along with unceasing demand explained why the "war on drugs" could never be won.

Fighting Black Liberation in Africa

The US imperial policy of backing anti-democratic militarist regimes was global and thus included Africa. Democracy, racial justice and development were strictly secondary concerns, as during both the Cold War and the GWOT the United States pursued a continuous policy of empowering violently reactionary regimes and opposing reform efforts.

The United States conflated localized issues and nationalist insurgencies in Africa with the larger American crusades against communism and alleged terrorists. US neo-liberal economic policies and support for warlords and military strongmen undermined quests for democracy and social justice in US African policy. The United States thus for decades, as historian Elizabeth Schmidt notes, "intervened in African conflicts, with disastrous results."

In the 1950s and 60s the progress of the American civil rights movement brought increased rhetorical pressure on the apartheid regimes of southern Africa, but little if any direct action was taken against them. In 1968, with the civil rights movement receding, Nixon condemned the black power movement and vilified racial equality protesters along with the Vietnam antiwar movement during his "law and order" campaign for the presidency. Nixon subsequently bolstered US support for the undemocratic apartheid regimes and got an assist from Congress, which in 1971 passed the Byrd Amendment (named for a powerful segregationist senator). The amendment exempted Rhodesia, which was 95 percent black but ruled by a white minority, from trade sanctions concerning strategic materials, mainly chrome.

Following Nixon's ouster in Watergate, Kissinger advocated US intervention in Angola, Guinea and Mozambique. Independence struggles were raging in the longtime Portuguese colonies amid the collapse in 1974 of the authoritarian-regime of Antonio Salazar, who ruled Portugal for decades bolstered by funding and support from the United States and NATO. US officials were keenly concerned about the future of the massive US military base in the Portuguese Azores Islands, which enabled the projection of American power in Europe, Africa and the Middle East.

The United States secured the base, bolstered apartheid South Africa--which was imperiled by the mounting black liberation struggles in the neighboring countries--and sent arms and mercenaries into Angola. The West African country was one site, however, in the immediate aftermath of the debacle in Vietnam where the US Congress cut off funding for the Ford-Kissinger effort to intervene in another foreign civil war.

Kissinger was apoplectic as he sought to counter Cuba, which had intervened militarily in support of the anti-colonial struggle in Guinea. The Cubans played a key role in forcing Portugal to abandon the colony and also had some 36,000 troops fighting on the side of the rebels in Angola. While the Cubans—who Kissinger wrongly believed acted purely as Soviet proxies, rather than being driven by the Castro regime's own revolutionary ethos—fought for the cause of decolonization, the United States and South Africa lined up behind reactionary forces. The Soviet and Cuban-backed MPLA won the struggle for Angola in 1975.

In the late 1970s, the dictates of crusading American anti-communism in the Cold War led to intense conflict in the Horn of Africa. Strategically located near the Red Sea and Indian Ocean and in close proximity to Middle East oil supplies, the Horn became the site of shifting alliances as well as a war in the Ogaden Desert in 1977-78. In the convoluted geopolitics of the Cold War, the USSR armed and assisted Ethiopia, a former US ally, while the Americans armed and allied with Somalia, a former Soviet ally.

Carter promoted a discourse of racial equality and human rights in southern Africa before the 1980 election enabled Reagan to usher in "constructive engagement." The accommodating new policy sought to check international pressure on apartheid South Africa. That same year, however, the white supremacist regime in Rhodesia, long backed by Britain and the United States, collapsed and transitioned to majority rule as Zimbabwe. A civil war replete with Cold War rivalries raged in neighboring Mozambique, killing more than a million people before it was settled in 1992.

The CIA and an Angolan faction allied with South Africa in opposition to the liberation struggle in the former German colony of Southwest Africa. With the Cubans again playing a major role, years of brutal struggle culminated in a negotiated settlement and creation of the new nation of Namibia in 1990.

Despite decades of US support, South Africa could no longer swim against the tide of black liberation. A widespread international campaign of economic boycott and sanctions threatened to cripple the apartheid regime. In the early 1990s transition to majority rule culminated with the decisive election of the African National Congress under Nelson Mandela. Liberated after 27 years of political imprisonment, Mandela was elected president of the new South Africa.

Following the end of the Cold War, US African policy in the 1990s centered on supporting dictators amenable to resource extraction and in compliance with the neo-liberal economic policies of the Washington consensus. Regional instability escalated in Somalia, as in other client states such as Zaire and Liberia, where the United States backed warlords and dictators rather than supporting economic and social justice. In Somalia civil society devolved into clan-based warfare, precipitating widespread famine in the East African country. In Operation Restore Hope, US and UN forces brought famine relief, but the operation became increasingly militarized as the foreign forces clashed with warlords over food supplies amid a nascent civil war.

In October 1993, with resentment growing against UN and US forces, which had fired on crowds and conducted airborne assaults against clans and religious leaders, the United States suffered the indignity of the "Black Hawk Down" incident in which angry Somalis shot down an American helicopter, killed 18 US soldiers and paraded some of the bodies through the streets of Mogadishu. The Americans had gone in "like Rambo," as the Eritrean president put it, and, as the Pentagon later acknowledged, "We just didn't expect to meet the kind of resistance we did."

US officials placed all the blame for the clash on the inherent savagery of the Somali "Skinnies" and unleashed an indiscriminate military assault killing several hundred men, women and children while devastating whole neighborhoods. In 1994 President Bill Clinton withdrew US forces as the UN terminated the relief operation, leaving Somalia plagued by civil war and famine.

Soured by the Somali affair, the Clinton administration backed by the Republican controlled Congress pursued a devastating policy of malignant indifference to a 1994 genocide in the Great Lakes region of Africa. In Rwanda, the Tutsi minority, though comprising less than 15 percent of the population, had nonetheless dominated administration of the Central African country for decades under Belgian colonial rule. In April the assassination of the majority Hutu president of Rwanda fueled fears of a return to minority Tutsi rule. Hutu gangs lashed out with genocidal violence, which ultimately took the lives of between 800,000 and one million Tutsi and moderate Hutus.

The Clinton administration did not simply ignore, but actually facilitated the genocide by demanding a UN withdrawal from the country in the midst of the crisis and otherwise discouraging a meaningful international response to the unfolding mass murder. The United States continued in the decades following the genocide to provide military aid and political support to the Rwandan regime of Paul Kagame, a Tutsi who had received US military training at Fort Leavenworth and may well have been responsible for the assassination that set off the genocide. Ruling with an iron fist, Kagame backed the US economic policy of resource extraction in the Great Lakes, where he acted as a regional aggressor, including repeated invasions of the Congo and support for deploying children as soldiers.

The GWOT and Escalating Imperialism in Africa

After September 11, 2001, the United States under the GWOT exaggerated supposed security threats and conflated localized political and ethnic conflicts with the international crusade against terrorism. Once President George W. Bush pronounced that the 9/11 attacks (discussed in the next chapter) necessitated a policy of global intervention, the United States stormed into Africa as in other regions of the world to bolster military regimes that would crack down on alleged Muslim terrorists while continuing to adhere to Western economic dictates. Countries rich in energy resources and willing to fight "Islamic terror" could be assured of receiving US aid and weapons.

US strategy and policies were not only imperial, but fundamentally flawed. About 40 percent of Africa could be counted as Muslim, mostly in North and West as well as the Horn of Africa, where some residents and insurgents did resent the United States for its various affronts to the Muslim world, though few had any connection with 9/11. Coordinated Al Qaeda attacks against US embassies in Kenya and Tanzania occurred in 1998, by which time the terror organization had relocated to Afghanistan. The United States, however, viewed virtually any Muslim political or insurgent activity in Africa as part of a broader global anti-American Islamic terror campaign rather than, as was often the case, a response to localized conflict.

Under the enabling framework of the GWOT, US global imperialism and militarism spiked to unprecedented levels in Africa and worldwide. US counterterrorism strategy embraced corrupt governments responsible for serious human rights abuses in North, East, West, and Central Africa as well the Horn. Oppressive regimes garnering US support under the GWOT included Ethiopia, Kenya, Chad, Burkina Faso, Burundi, Nigeria, Uganda, Rwanda, South Sudan and Congo. In the time-honored tradition, Washington brought African militarists to the United States for "security" training, where they quickly learned that if they agreed to identify and combat "Islamic terrorists," military supplies, crucial US political support, and personal enrichment would soon follow.

US military intervention and support for dictators further alienated many Africans rather than the supposed counterinsurgency goal of winning their hearts and minds. As Schmidt points out, "Rather than promoting security, US military and covert operations often intensified strife and undermined prospects for peace" on the continent.

The American imperial "footprint" escalated dramatically as the United States put thousands of boots on the ground and established military bases and facilities throughout the African continent. Djibouti, strategically located at the juncture of the Red Sea and Gulf of Aden, was developed as a pivotal US counterterrorism base in Africa. The United States sought out bases, ports and other facilities in Algeria, Gabon, Kenya, Mali, Morocco, Namibia, Senegal, Tunisia, Uganda and Zambia.

Military programs displaced humanitarian efforts, as the Pentagon shouldered aside US and international agencies pursuing development and social progress. To its credit, the George W. Bush administration did pump billions of dollars, albeit funneled through profit-taking Big Pharma corporations, into the effort to contain the HIV AIDS epidemic, but otherwise relatively little was done for health and welfare on the African continent.

While some might expect that Barack Obama, an African American whose father was Kenyan, might take a different approach, in fact his administration maintained a continuous US policy under the GWOT. During Obama's two terms US national security elites continued to dispense American largesse based on access to resources--especially oil, natural gas and uranium—and to view localized political and economic conflicts as part of a broader "Islamic terror" movement. Obama sharply increased US covert operations and especially drone attacks, with Somalia serving as the principal African target.

Elected in 2016, Trump displayed contempt for Muslims and advocated a vague "America first" foreign policy, but he did not bring a halt to US intervention in Africa. The Trump administration emphasized trade and resource extraction and maintained the US imperial and military presence in part because of concern about growing Chinese involvement in Africa. Trump's overall racist indifference to what he called the "shithole countries" of Africa led to an even sharper decline in humanitarian assistance and diplomatic engagement, as he cut funding and refused to fill relevant positions in the State Department.

Fallout from the Cold War

The collapse of the Cold War order precipitated dramatic changes in Eastern Europe. The worst fallout occurred in the former Yugoslavia, which functioned for decades as a stable communist regime under Josip Broz Tito, but in the 1990s devolved into bitter ethnic and religious separatism and conflict. The United States responded first with confusion, then with diplomacy, and finally with a characteristic paroxysm of militarism.

After Croatia and Slovenia moved to establish independent republics, Serbs unleashed ethnic cleansing operations, which drove more than a million Bosnian Muslims and Croats from their homes. Pitiless Serbian militarists then laid siege to the historic Bosnian city of Sarajevo. Serbs were aggressors but also victims as Croats, Bosnian Muslims and others lashed out as the ethnic conflicts spiraled out of control.

The UN intervened ineffectively while the first Bush administration remained aloof, with Secretary of State James Baker explaining, "We don't have a dog in that fight." In 1994 Clinton collaborated with the Western Europeans to engage NATO, which had become an alliance in search of a mission in the wake of the dissolution of the USSR. A limited NATO bombing campaign arrested the siege of Sarajevo after which the United States brokered the Dayton Accords (1995) at a US airbase in Ohio. The settlement sanctioned the creation of new states along ethnic lines and ended the violent cleansing operations replete with rape houses and the slaughter of civilians. War crimes trials ensued.

In 1999 ethnic Albanians sought separation in the province of Kosovo, which the Serbs had long considered sacred ground and therefore went on the offensive to retain. Under the NATO command of US General Wesley Clark, the United States responded with a 78-day campaign of intensive bombing, carrying out some 38,000 sorties. The punitive bombing pummeled Serbia into submission and paved the way for the eventual independence of Kosovo.

The US-led bombing was illegal under international law as it was unsanctioned by the UN Security Council and opposed by India, China and the new Russia, among others. The punishing campaign caused some $100 billion dollars damage, taking out schools, hospitals, roads, bridges, and historic buildings, killing and wounding thousands of people and displacing perhaps a million others. On May 7 five US guided bombs struck the Chinese embassy in Belgrade, killing three people, an attack that most Chinese to this day refuse to believe was, as the United States apologetically insisted, unintentional.

Aside from relentlessly bombing the Serbs, NATO found purpose by expanding into former Soviet territory and thereby rekindling the flames of the Cold War. Thus, despite the US claim to having won a transcendent victory in the Cold War, the conflict with Russia did not come to an end, primarily as a result of American arrogance and imperial expansion.

Beginning in the mid-1980s, the Soviet leader Mikhail Gorbachev had tried to reform the USSR through economic restructuring and the enabling of freedom of speech, but the former failed and the latter precipitated such widespread condemnation of past Communist Party abuses that the Union lost legitimacy and collapsed in 1991. After some hesitation, the United States embraced the inept Boris Yeltsin as the new leader, but the Russian Federation descended into chaos and deep-seated corruption. US-led neo-liberalism complemented the efforts of Russian oligarchs to plunder state resources for themselves while the economic conditions for masses of people sharply deteriorated. In 2000 Vladimir Putin, the former head of the KGB security police, won election and gradually reestablished an autocratic government in which he became essentially the new tsar.

The United States spurred the considerable popular support that Putin attained in Russia by choosing imperial expansion over economic assistance and a more calibrated cultivation of the new Russia. In the 1990s the United States chose to expand NATO—an anti-Russian military alliance--by incorporating the former Soviet republics in the Baltic States as well as former allied nations in Eastern Europe including Poland, Hungary, Romania and the Czech Republic.

George Kennan, the original architect of the containment policy, warned at the time that NATO expansion would inflame "the nationalistic, anti-Western and militaristic tendencies in Russian opinion . . . restore the atmosphere of the Cold War to East-West relations" and would be "a strategic blunder of epic proportions." Kennan was right.

Rather than choosing a new relationship with the briefly democratic Russia—even a new Marshall Plan might have been appropriate—the United States led its Western European allies to extend a hostile alliance, igniting Russian fears of encirclement. "By denying Russia the prospect of eventual NATO membership while Central Europe and the Baltic states joined," political scientist Angela Stent points out, "America reinforced the Kremlin's belief that it remains outside of Euro-Atlantic structures and hence has no responsibility to them."

Having supported both the Persian Gulf War and the GWOT, Russia also felt double crossed when the United States did not support the Second Chechen War, which Russia claimed was part of the war on terror.

At the same time, the United States further extended its influence along Russia's borders by opening new military bases in former Soviet Central Asia. The Americans refused to compromise on anti-missile defense development and site expansion, though the United States and Russia did wisely come to terms on other nuclear arms control accords.

The renewed Cold War rivals clashed over US support for an illegitimate and sharply anti-Russian Ukrainian government that ousted its elected predecessor in an American-backed coup. The Russians responded by taking control of the Crimean Peninsula, predominated by ethnic Russians, and waging a war with Ukraine over the ethnically divided Donbass region of Ukraine. The United States and Russia also engaged in continuous propaganda, disinformation and destabilizing cyber warfare, though the US national media focused only the Russian side of these activities, rarely inquiring into the American ones.

Aided by lucrative oil and natural gas sales, Putin reinforced his power and proved to be an unsavory but cunning adversary of the United States. Many Russians blamed the Americans and their Western allies for the collapse of the USSR, the plundering of Russian resources, and for the efforts to isolate and undermine Russia in order to deprive it of its rightful status as a great power. Russia--like Hungary and Poland among other newly proclaimed and supposedly "free world" countries of Eastern Europe--remained an authoritarian regime.

A critical country spanning Europe and Asia and with a seat on the UN Security Council, the new Russia could have been cultivated as a partner for cooperation on a variety of crucial global issues. The United States instead showed complete disdain for Russian interests as well as Russian pride and thus squandered the prospects of a establishing a productive post Cold War relationship.

Chapter 9
Imperialism and Endless Wars in the Middle East

In the wake of World War II American imperialism migrated to the Middle East (West Asia). Oil, Zionism, arms sales and arrogance fueled the imperial march, which left the region more militarized and unstable than ever, and the United States mired in an endless cycle of war. While not widely recognized as such, US Middle East policy was arguably as disastrous as the Indochina war.

The United States had only marginal involvement with the Middle East before the postwar era. In the early seventeenth century the first American militarist, John Smith, had fought the Islamic "Moors" in southeastern Europe before migrating west and setting his sights on ethnic cleansing in Virginia. In the early 1800s the young United States sent warships to battle Islamic pirates on the "Barbary Coast" of North Africa. More than century later, after World War I, the United States supported the perpetuation of European colonialism in the former territories of the Ottoman Empire.

World War II underscored the importance of oil to modern militarism and to industrial societies, thus ensuring that the United States would stake a dominant claim. Two months before his death in April 1945, President Roosevelt hosted the founding monarch of Saudi Arabia, Abd al-Aziz Ibn Saud, aboard ship in North Africa, thus inaugurating what would become one of the most critical relationships in postwar history. The essence of the relationship, which endured for the next 75 years, at least, was an exchange of American access to cheap Saudi oil in return for ensuring the security of the autocracy.

After World War II, US policy centered on providing political and military support for oil-producers, not just in Saudi Arabia but throughout the Persian Gulf. US policy thus bolstered some of the most reactionary regimes in the world--as long as they were anti-communist and kept the oil flowing at an affordable price. The Saudi and other governments of the region shared the oil wealth but remained dependent on foreign corporate consortiums like Aramco, closely tied in with the US national security state, to provide the extraction, refining, distribution and sale of petroleum.

By 1950 millions of barrels of oil were flowing from the Gulf into the US-dominated global economic system. Over time the United States, Western Europe and Japan became increasingly dependent on Middle East oil.

After the Roosevelt and Truman administrations laid the foundation for perpetual US intervention in the Middle East, Eisenhower went a step further. Having been the wartime leader of a massive, oil-dependent allied coalition, Eisenhower well understood the critical importance of the petroleum pipeline. Under his direction in 1953 the United States colluded with the British in the overthrow of the democratically elected Mossadegh government in Iran (discussed in Chapter 7).

The coup in Iran was a signature event that underscored the US dedication to support autocracy rather than democracy in the Gulf region while at the same time laying the foundation for massive blowback against the United States beginning some 25 years later and carrying to the present day. At the time, however, the CIA coup kept the oil flowing and the repressive monarchies backed by corporate power and the US security state remained intact.

American-Backed Zionism

In addition to the drive to access cheap oil, decisive US support for Zionism has profoundly influenced Middle East policy. The growing American commitment to support the new Israel--a predominately European settler colonial state implanted in the center of the Arab world--fueled tensions in the region, thus spurring the American imperialism and militarism that have been required to manage the fallout.

Founded around the turn of the century, Zionism—the quest for a Jewish homeland in Palestine—grew through the migration of European settlers who received crucial endorsement from the British Balfour Declaration (1917), which in turn was endorsed by the United States. In the 1930s and 1940s Jews who migrated in large numbers from Europe amid the Nazi pogroms and ultimately amid the Nazi genocide clashed with Palestinian Arabs and with British mandate authorities. The British supported the Zionists in repressing an Arab revolt against the mass European migration into Palestine in the late 1930s. However, the Jewish settlers turned against the British during World War II, as they strove to establish an independent state. Palestinian Arabs also sought an internationally recognized state.

Weakened by the war, British power receded, including abandoning its colonial mandate in Palestine, which the newly created UN partitioned in

145

1947. The UN thus provided an international legal foundation for the creation of Israel the following year.

The support of the United States, which became the first nation in the world to offer de facto recognition of Israel, was crucial. From that point forward the United States, which had the largest Jewish population in the world at the time, became the chief supporter of Israel, which expanded its territory as it drove some 750,000 Palestinians from their homes and lands in the 1948 war. In September of that year Zionist terrorists assassinated at a Jerusalem roadblock Count Folke Bernadotte of Sweden, who had been dispatched by the UN to mediate the conflict. Israel thereafter remained consistently contemptuous of the UN.

In domestic politics a powerful Israel lobby reinforced American cultural support for Israel, which found roots in religion—Protestant as well as Jewish--and mutual histories of settler colonization. By the end of the Truman administration the US Congress, pressed by the nascent lobby, was instituting a regular program of financial support. Israel, a small country of some nine million people today, would become by far the largest recipient of US foreign assistance in all of American history. Not coincidentally, the American Israel Public Affairs Committee (AIPAC) at the same time became easily the most powerful lobby advocating the interests of a foreign country in American history, and one of the most powerful lobbies in Washington, period.

The American largesse enabled Israel to become a military powerhouse and a regional aggressor backed by the leading power in the world. Israel's congenital aggression played out in borderland attacks on Jordan and Syria as well in 1956 the tripartite invasion of Egypt in collusion with Britain and France. Kept out of the loop, the United States demanded a withdrawal from the Sinai Peninsula, with Israel refusing to vacate Egyptian territory until it received as a reward for its aggression new navigation rights in the Gulf of Aqaba.

Israel's support in the US Congress continued to grow, enabling it to fend off UN requirements to repatriate or otherwise compensate Palestinian refugees driven from their homes in the 1948 *Nakba* (The Catastrophe) and to ensure that Jerusalem remained, as the UN mandated, an international city. The Zionists claimed it as their own "eternal capital." Israel also defied and repeatedly misled the United States by developing nuclear weapons, in an open secret that has never been officially acknowledged.

In 1966 and 1967 Israel launched major cross-border attacks on Jordan as well as Syria, which prompted Egyptian President Gamal Abdul Nasser, the titular leader of the Arab world, to oust UN occupation forces on the Sinai Peninsula and renounce Israel's navigation rights in the Gulf of Aqaba. In June 1967 Israel seized the opportunity to go on the offensive by attacking its Arab neighbors in the Six-Day War. President Johnson urged Israel not to attack but ultimately acquiesced to the aggression and stood ready to come to Israel's support if necessary.

The administration overlooked the apparently deliberate Israeli attack on an American spy ship, the USS *Liberty*, which was monitoring the war. Israel claimed that the air and sea-borne attack in international waters on the defenseless ship, which killed 34 sailors and wounded 171 others, was accidental, but that version of events was widely rejected within the US Government, including the CIA. Israel may have feared the ship's reporting would preclude an impending attack on Syria or expose the execution of Egyptian soldiers, no one can say for sure in the absence of a determined investigation, which has never occurred.

More powerful militarily than the neighboring Arab states combined, Israel crushed Egypt, Jordan and Syria in the six days of war, seizing the Sinai Peninsula from Egypt, the Golan Heights from Syria, and the West Bank of the Jordan River from Jordan. Israel had positioned itself to trade these territories back, as the UN mandated in Security Council Resolution 242 (1968), in return for peace with the Arabs, which had to that point refused to recognize the Zionist state. Israel chose instead to solidify its illegal occupation and establish colonial authority over the newly occupied territories.

In October 1973 Egypt, now led by Anwar Sadat, launched a surprise attack against Israel. The Zionist state was reeling until Nixon and Kissinger responded with massive arms shipments, which helped turn the trajectory of the war. Allied with Egypt, the Soviet Union threatened intervention in order to get the Israelis to halt their offensive, which prompted the United States to go onto nuclear alert status (Defcon 3).

The Arab Oil Embargo

At this point the US balancing act of supporting the oil-rich Arab monarchies while at the same time providing unstinting support for the "Zionist entity" that they detested reached a tipping point. In 1960 several of the oil-producing states had come together in the formation of the Organization of Petroleum Exporting Countries (OPEC) in order to drive up the price of crude. Now, in the wake of US resupply of Israel in the October 1973 war, the Arab oil producers led by the chief US client Saudi Arabia, slapped an embargo on oil shipments to the United States.

The OPEC embargo underscored Western dependency and fueled an economic crisis of "stagflation"—both stagnation and inflation--in the 1970s. American consumers fumed over long lines and record high prices at the gas pumps. The OPEC countries took more control over the production process, with the Saudis eventually nationalizing the former Aramco holdings in 1980.

The United States neither backed off its support for imperial Israel nor for the oil-soaked Arab monarchies, which they instead coopted through arms sales as well as ongoing political support. The consequences of US imperialism in the region thus did not lead to retraction and rethinking, but rather to increased militarization and stepped-up support for repressive regimes, Arab as well as Zionist.

Under the Nixon Doctrine, pronounced in 1971, the United States vowed that rather than intervening directly in countries such as Vietnam it would in the future arm its clients to the teeth to defend themselves as well as American interests. Applying the new doctrine to the Middle East, the Arab states as well as Iran proved eager to use their vast oil-producing wealth to buy American advanced weaponry. With Iran and Saudi Arabia as the leading purchasers, the United States sold billions of dollars-worth of high-tech weaponry including fighter jets to the Middle East autocrats. The Soviet Union participated at a lower level, further militarizing the unstable region.

Well aware of the arms sales to the Arabs and Iran, Israel in turn demanded the most advanced weapons on the most favorable terms in order to remain militarily superior to the surrounding Arabs. Lobbied intensively, the Congress proved willing even as Israel continued to refuse to negotiate over the illegal occupation, which included seizing control of Jerusalem, the third holiest site in Islam after Mecca and Medina in Saudi Arabia.

The military-industrial complex, the Israelis, and the oil-producing autocracies were all big winners in the American-brokered pernicious solution of escalating repression and militarization in one of the world's most volatile regions. The military regime in Egypt went along and went alone, as Sadat negotiated a separate peace with Israel securing the return of the Sinai in return for recognition in 1979.

Despite Jimmy Carter's efforts at Camp David, Maryland, the previous year, Israel under the reactionary leadership of Menachem Begin, who was dedicated to annexing the biblical Israel, again rejected the chance for a broader peace, including the creation of a Palestinian state. The United States, especially under Reagan and his successors, rewarded Israeli colonialism and apartheid rule over Palestinians with unprecedented funding and military collaboration.

Implosion

Failing to promote peace or security much less democratization, American imperialism instead laid the groundwork for the massive blowback that materialized with the Iranian Revolution of 1979. The roots for the Iranian revolt lay in the 1953 coup, which the British and the Americans had covertly orchestrated in order not only to retain control of Iranian oil but also to eliminate the example of a progressive government exercising even partial control, which was all that Mossadegh had sought, over its own resources and mainly oil.

Reza Pahlavi, the Shah of Iran, whom the Americans and the British had put on the throne after the coup ousting Mossadegh, alienated Iranians through his repressive rule, which had long been reinforced by a ruthless state police force, the SAVAK. While compiling one of the most egregious human rights records in the world, replete with torture and liberal use of the death penalty, the Shah also carried out the "White Revolution." The showcasing program of modernization alienated many Iranians, including Islamic fundamentalists, who came to power under the formerly exiled cleric Ayatollah Khomeini. When Carter allowed the Shah, riddled with cancer, into the United States for treatment, "students" took over the US Embassy in Tehran, which they occupied while humiliating the Americans for the next 444 days.

The Iranian Revolution as well as unrest in Saudi Arabia, which was rocked by two major rebellions in 1979 before they were repressed, underscored the failure of the US neo-imperial policy of maintaining stability and the flow of oil by arming the regional autocracies. In addition to the collapse of Iran, Carter grappled with the fallout from the Soviet invasion of neighboring Afghanistan in December 1979. In a perfervid response, Cold War elites charged that the assault was the first wave of a red tide to seize control of the entire Persian Gulf, but in reality, the Kremlin was clamping down in Afghanistan out of concern that the Islamic uprisings in Iran as well as Afghanistan would migrate and inflame Soviet Central Asia.

Carter played into the rising Cold War hysteria by making the hyperbolic claim in his January 1980 State of the Union address that the Soviet attack in Afghanistan represented "the most serious threat to world peace since the Second World War," as if the Korean War, Berlin war scares and the Cuban Missile Crisis had never occurred. Asserting his own "doctrine," the former proponent of peace and human rights announced that the United States would use "any means necessary, including military force" to safeguard its "vital interests" in the Persian Gulf.

The Carter Doctrine signaled the failure of the Nixon Doctrine, which had depended on arming surrogates to protect perceived US interests, and it marked the beginning of at least 40 years of direct US military intervention in the region. Consumed by the hostage crisis, Carter authorized a high-risk mission flying across the desert into Tehran to rescue the captives. In April 1980 mechanical and logistical problems resulted in the mission being aborted, at which point the debacle culminated with the crash of a transport helicopter killing eight US soldiers.

The enduring hostage crisis, as well as the Afghan invasion and ongoing economic problems, doomed the Carter presidency and propelled American politics in a right-wing direction. Long considered too extreme to become president owing to Barry Goldwater's landslide defeat in 1964, Reagan capitalized on the crises while some of his supporters worked behind the scenes to promise Khomeini renewed US weaponry if he held off on releasing the hostages until after the election. Reagan crushed Carter in the 1980 election, taking office on the day all of the hostages came home. The right wing of the Republican Party, formerly viewed as beyond the mainstream, would powerfully influence American politics for at least the next 40 years. Imperialism, once again, helped undermine the prospects for reform at home as the country veered sharply to the right.

Reagan, who as president of the Screen Actors Guild in the early Cold War orchestrated the purge of leftists from Hollywood, was now dedicated to hyper-aggressive waging of the global Cold War. He thus orchestrated a series of disastrous Middle East interventions. He escalated an initiative begun under Carter to arm Islamic fundamentalists to disrupt the Soviet effort to reassert authority in Afghanistan. "The Islamic world had not seen an armed jihad for centuries," anthropologist Mahmood Mamdani has pointed out. "But now the CIA was determined to create one." Reagan welcomed into the Oval Office a group of the *mujahedin*—reactionary Islamists funded primarily by the Saudi regime—and praised them as "freedom fighters" on a par with the American founding fathers. The CIA equipped the Islamist resistance with weapons notably shoulder-fired Stinger missiles, which exacted a heavy toll on the Soviet occupation forces.

By the end of the 1980s the Soviets withdrew from Afghanistan in defeat amid the general disintegration of the USSR. The United States declared victory and turned Afghanistan over to the reactionary Islamists, the Taliban, setting the stage for another round of devastating blowback a little more than a decade later.

Decimating Lebanon

Having rejected Carter's effort at Camp David to forge a solution of the Palestine conflict, the right-wing Israeli Likud Party under Begin announced a unilateral and patently illegal annexation of the Syrian Golan Heights. Israel also bombed an Iraqi nuclear research site though Iraq was nowhere near developing nuclear weapons, as Israel itself covertly had done while refusing to sign the 1968 Nonproliferation Treaty. The Reagan administration admonished the Israelis but took no meaningful action in response to their aggression, which ensured that more would follow.

In 1982 Reagan's Secretary of State General Alexander Haig green-lighted an Israeli invasion of Lebanon, where the Palestine Liberation Organization was headquartered. In addition to the effort to destroy the PLO, Israel had long desired to ensconce a friendly Maronite Christian regime in neighboring Lebanon. When that plan imploded as a result of the assassination of the Maronite leader, Israeli Defense Minister Ariel Sharon--a confirmed war criminal responsible for the 1953 Qibya massacre in Jordan--enabled and then attempted to cover up a murderous rampage by the Christian militia at the Sabra and Shatila Palestinian refugee camps in which some 2,000 people were slaughtered. Meanwhile for weeks Israel shelled and bombed Beirut, the proverbial Paris of the Middle East, causing massive destruction and killing some 20,000 Lebanese.

Israel characteristically ignored US and UN demands for a ceasefire, prompting Reagan to authorize an ill-conceived US military intervention in Lebanon. Left exposed and without a clear mission, US forces promptly became sitting ducks for two devastating attacks. In April 1983 a suicide bomber slammed a pickup truck into the US Embassy in Beirut, killing 63 people including 17 Americans. On October 23, 241 US Marines along with 58 French soldiers died in another truck bomb attack near the Beirut airport.

The United States thus paid the price in the blowback assaults that stemmed from the enabling of Israeli aggression, support for which had been strengthened by the beefed-up Israel lobby on the home front. Reagan ignominiously withdrew the US forces that he had recklessly committed and left vulnerable in Beirut. Meanwhile, the administration and the lobby stepped up military assistance to Israel even as it carried out a construction boom throughout the 1980s with the building of illegal Jewish-only settlements in the occupied Palestinian territories, thus deepening the conflict with the Arabs.

Israel's foray into Lebanon had been a disaster. Instead of establishing a friendly government on its northern border Israel spurred the creation of Hizbullah, an Iranian and Syrian-backed yet homegrown Shi'ite insurgency in Lebanon. Motivated by both the Israeli and the American failed operations in Lebanon, the resistance fighters dug into the southern hills, built enough popular support to enter into Lebanese politics, and became a permanent force that the Israelis could rail against, yet were unable to defeat. Israel, like its benefactor, had thus created its own blowback.

Reagan's militarized Middle East policy continued in Libya, whose autocratic leader, Muammar Gaddafi, had long been a thorn in the American side. In 1981 the Reagan administration deliberately stoked conflict over disputed airspace with Libya, which had been one of many sponsors of the various hijackings, kidnappings and attacks on US facilities that blew back on Americans in the 1980s. In 1986 the United States, blaming Libya for the bombing of a discotheque frequented by Americans in West Berlin, carried out a flawed bombing operation, which damaged the French embassy in Tripoli but failed to achieve its unacknowledged goal of assassinating Gaddafi, whom Reagan had labeled "the mad dog of the Middle East."

On Dec. 21, 1988, the devastating blowback for the clash with Libya came when Gaddafi's agents planted a bomb, which exploded over Lockerbie, Scotland, killing all 259 passengers on Pan American Flight 103.

Fueling War with Iran and Iraq

In 1980 the Iraqi dictator Saddam Hussein launched an invasion of neighboring Iran. Intent on precluding a Shi'ite uprising from spreading to Iraq, Hussein also hoped to capitalize on Iran's revolutionary turmoil and its loss of US military backing. A brutal war raged until 1988, killing hundreds of thousands of people and destabilizing the entire region.

The United States spurred the conflict by offering military aid to both sides and even condoning Iraq's use of chemical weapons, some against its own people. US military forces continued to come in harm's way. In May 1987 the Reagan administration accepted Iraq's apology after its mistaken attack on the USS *Stark*, a Navy frigate, killing 37 sailors and injuring 21 others. Military aid to Iran ended after revelations of the Iran-Contra affair and failed efforts to trade weapons for kidnapped Western hostages.

By the late 1980s the United States was waging an undeclared war with Iran, which the Americans identified as the primary rogue state bogeyman in the region. The Saudis and other reactionary monarchies wore the white hats in American eyes though they funded jihad and brutally repressed their own populations. Determined to maintain the stability and flow of oil from the Gulf autocracies, the United States in 1986 began reflagging of oil tankers for the reactionary monarchy in Kuwait, deepening direct US involvement in the volatile Gulf.

In 1987 US and Iranian forces clashed directly, including the US sinking of several Iranian warships. In July 1988 the USS *Vincennes* recklessly shot down an Iranian civilian airbus, killing all 290 people aboard. Washington absurdly blamed the civilian aircraft for the incident.

Iran accepted a ceasefire ending the war with Iraq in 1988, but Hussein chose to start yet another war, this one with Kuwait. The war with Iran left Iraq deeply indebted and unable to revive its collapsed economy. With his regime on the ropes, Hussein demanded debt relief from his Arab lenders and a reduction in world oil supplies in order to spur a price increase. Neighboring Kuwait, whose arbitrary borders with Iraq had been drawn generations before by British imperialists, showed no sympathy for Hussein's demands, prompting the Iraqi militarist to invade the country in August 1990.

The George H.W. Bush administration famously drew a "line in the sand" over the military assault while exaggerating the threat that Iraq, which had been unable to subdue Iran, would nonetheless be able to follow up the sacking of Kuwait by invading and controlling Saudi Arabia. In a deliberate reversal of incremental escalation in Vietnam, the United States amassed a massive invasion force, which it unleashed in January 1991 after the Iraqis rejected the ultimatum to pull out of Kuwait.

Americans gloried in the ensuing paroxysm of militarism in which they summarily crushed Saddam's forces in the 1991 Persian Gulf War. The United States unleashed nearly 100,000 bombing sorties and more than 300 Cruise missile attacks, followed by a coordinated ground assault. The unambiguous military victory brought psychic relief that lingered from the humiliations of Vietnam and the 444-day Iran hostage crisis. "By God, we've kicked the Vietnam Syndrome once and for all," gushed Bush. "The American people fell in love again with their armed forces," added General Colin Powell.

Combined with the Soviet collapse, the crushing victory prompted the self-absorbed Americans once again proudly to proclaim their global supremacy. But military victory alone accomplishes little, as Clausewitz might have reminded the giddy US commanders. In reality, decades of wrenching blowback lay ahead.

As it geared up for the war the United States had flooded Saudi Arabia with some 107,000 US troops. The little-known Osama bin Laden, the *mujahedin* leader from an elite Saudi family, was among those outraged at the monarchy for welcoming the hordes of Zionist-supporting infidels into the holy land to fight a war that he believed should have been won without them.

The horrific humanitarian situation the Americans created in Iraq was another source of widespread Arab and Islamic resentment that would fuel decades of blowback assaults. While the Bush administration ruled out removing Saddam from power, it invited Iraq's Shi'ite majority and Kurdish minority to overthrow the secular Sunni strongman on their own. However, when they tried to do so, the Americans sat back and thus enabled their slaughter by Saddam's regime. US national security elites did not want to see Iraq's Shi'ite majority come to power and to ally with the similarly constituted Iran, but they had created in Iraq an "epic humanitarian disaster and a huge embarrassment for the United Sates," as historian Andrew Bacevich has pointed out.

Washington responded by instituting a regime of sanctions that were supposed to rein in Saddam, but at the same time they further undermined an already devastated Iraqi economy and society. From 1991 to 2003 the United States flew tens of thousands of sorties, interspersed with occasional bombings and Cruise missile attacks, as it policed a massive "no-fly zone," in effect an air occupation, to preclude Saddam's attacks on his own population. Meanwhile hundreds of thousands of Iraqis died amid the economic and medical crisis that had been inflicted on the country.

Beyond liberating a reactionary monarchy in Kuwait and making itself feel better in the process, the United States had achieved little in the Persian Gulf War. The region remained roiled by conflict and human suffering that the Americans had made much worse in Iraq. Resentment over Western intrusions combined with backwardness, corruption as well as the ongoing Israeli settlement and occupation of Arab territories, including Jerusalem, left the region in which the United States was deeply embedded in a highly combustible state.

Bush had tried to push the Israelis to enter into meaningful peace talks, but the Zionist state instead repressed the Palestinian Intifada, an effort that had erupted in 1987 to "shake off" the occupation. Forced kicking and screaming into the Oslo "peace process," Israel throughout the 1990s stonewalled the effort to create a viable Palestinian state. Zionist settlers continued to establish more facts on the ground that increasingly made a two-state solution unachievable. The Israel lobby continued to police any domestic US effort to rein in Israel, which remained the largest recipient of foreign military assistance and the most powerful military in the Middle East thanks to its superpower benefactor.

By the early 1990s bin Laden and his Al Qaeda jihadi movement were committed to attacking the "Zionist-Crusader alliance." In February 1993 Al Qaeda exploded a bomb in a van parked in a garage at the World Trade Center in New York, injuring about a thousand people and doing $500 million in damage. The "Black Hawk down" debacle in Somalia the following year, which according to bin Laden had shown "weakness, frailty and cowardice of the US troops," encouraged his growing conviction that the United States was a "paper tiger" that could successfully be attacked.

In 1996 bin Laden issued a manifesto directing followers to kill Americans whenever possible and drive them from "all the lands of Islam." In June a truck bomb struck an apartment complex housing US personnel near an American air base in Dhahran, Saudi Arabia, killing 19 US soldiers. On Aug. 7, 1998--the precise day chosen to mark the eighth anniversary of the arrival of US troops in the Saudi homeland—Al Qaeda perpetrated deadly bombings at the US embassies in Kenya and Tanzania. Hundreds of people, though only 12 of them American, were killed and thousands injured in the two attacks. The Clinton administration responded by firing some 70 Tomahawk missiles on sites in Afghanistan and in Sudan. None struck meaningful targets and one exploded a pharmaceutical plant in Khartoum falsely believed to be manufacturing chemical weapons. On October 12, 2000, an Al Qaeda bomb struck the USS *Cole*, left vulnerable at anchor in Aden, Yemen, killing 17 sailors and wounding dozens more.

The shattering September 11, 2001, attacks, perpetrated by Al Qaeda, ignited a crusading rage that would propel the United States into a series of senseless and ultimately fruitless wars. The 9/11 attacks created a domestic climate conducive to mobilizing widespread public support behind a protean campaign to forcibly remake the world to American liking.

Even before September 11, the United States was moving toward launching all-out campaigns of regime change in what became the Global War on Terror (GWOT). Since "victory" in the Cold War and the Persian Gulf War, increasingly empowered neo-conservatives advocated direct intervention to promote Western economic supremacy and to topple "rogue" governments. As the Project for a New American Century put it in 1997, rather than respond to events the United States should act aggressively "to shape a new century favorable to American principles and interests."

Within hours of the devastating 9/11 hijacked airliner attacks felling the twin towers of the World Trade Center in New York and smashing the Pentagon, the George W. Bush administration decided, as Defense Secretary Donald Rumsfeld put it, to "go massive—sweep it all up, things related and not." The myriad targets for intervention that ensued did not, however, include Saudi Arabia, from which 15 of the 19 suicide hijackers had emanated. The Bush administration spirited Saudi elites out of Washington before they could be questioned and thereafter deflected attention away from the oil-soaked regime, which had been funding jihadi activities across the globe.

While shielding Saudi Arabia and other reactionary Gulf regimes, the official US investigation blamed poor intelligence by the FBI and CIA for the 9/11 attacks, thus enabling the creation of a vast new "national security" bureaucracy, the Department of Homeland Security, to oversee alleged threats, domestic as well as international. The 9/11 attacks thus spurred explosive growth in the already metastasizing US national security state.

Waging the GWOT

Bush, who unlike his father was a complete novice in foreign affairs and thus putty in the hands of Rumsfeld and Vice President Dick Cheney, pronounced a series of childishly simplistic yet sweeping assessments reducing complex international realities to a morality play of good versus evil. "Every nation, in every region, now has a decision to make," he declaimed on September 20. "Either you are with us, or you are with the terrorists."

As often occurred throughout the sweep of American history, wartime hysteria led to an erosion of civil liberties on the home front. Rammed into law in the perfervid atmosphere that prevailed 45 days after the 9/11 attacks, the USA Patriot Act--an even less subtle moniker than Roosevelt's H.R. 1776—launched the first of a series of changes to surveillance laws enabling the national security state to spy on individual Americans' phone and email communications, bank records, and internet search activity.

As in World War I and the Cold War, among other occasions, "national security" again trumped constitutional rights. Over the ensuing years whistle blowers such as Julian Assange, Chelsea Manning and Edward Snowden, who leaked evidence of illegal domestic and foreign surveillance, among other nefarious activities, were condemned and indicted by the US secrecy and security regime. Assange and Manning were jailed while Snowden escaped into exile in Russia.

With the US public stunned and angered by the wrenching scenes of the fallen towers, the nation was primed once again to unleash its military might. The United States struck first in Afghanistan, where it had been primarily responsible for funding and arming the global jihadi movement in the first place. US forces aligned with the Northern Alliance and looked the other way as the new allies starved and slaughtered civilians as they helped drive from power the Taliban, who had provided safe haven to bin Laden and other *mujahedin*. Heavily bombed and besieged in his hideout in the Tora Bora Mountains, bin Laden narrowly escaped into neighboring

Pakistan where he would spend another decade attempting to torment the Americans before they finally hunted down and killed him in 2011.

With its sights already set on another invasion of Iraq, the United States abandoned Afghanistan to a weak government that enjoyed little popular support beyond Kabul. The Taliban reverted to guerrilla resistance and quickly rebuilt from the initial American and Northern Alliance onslaught. The US intervention in Afghanistan thus accomplished little besides laying the foundation for decades of blowback that would translate into the longest war in American history.

In his Jan. 29, 2002, State of the Union address, Bush pronounced the "axis of evil" lumping Iran, Iraq and now nuclear armed North Korea as regimes that should be overthrown. The administration thus articulated a policy of preemption arrogating to the all-supreme United States the right to wage wars of regime change despite the absence of direct provocation. North Korea and Iran could cause major damage to an attacker, however, whereas Iraq was already under containment and thus ripe for the kill.

Deploying a strategy of disinformation, the Bush administration trumpeted Iraqi efforts to develop weapons of mass destruction as the *casus belli*. Lacking evidence to support this mendacious claim, the administration resorted to a massive a propaganda campaign emphasizing the supposed Iraqi threat as a cover for its own desire to launch a preemptive war to assert US hegemony backed by "full-spectrum dominance" militarism.

Rather than allow UN inspections to continue, the Bush administration launched another massive "shock and awe" campaign against the vulnerable Islamic nation in March 2003. Most of the American public initially backed the war, though protests erupted nationwide and in some cases were repressed by police. In any case, they drew little coverage from a news media anxious to display its patriotic bona fides rather than be accused as in the Vietnam era of siding with the enemy and war protesters. Unlike the first assault on Iraq, the 2003 attack lacked UN and international support beyond Great Britain and the few other countries that comprised a paltry "coalition of the willing."

Once again, the military victory was the easy part. The ensuing occupation proved to be an unmitigated disaster. Walled off in the safety of the "green zone," the United States alienated masses of Iraqis, including former members of the military and officials of the disbanded Ba'ath Party. The size of the US occupation force was insufficient to prevent massive looting or moreover to control access to weaponry. The United States thus created the perfect scenario for an enduring armed insurgency, which duly followed.

The occupation alienated Iraqis rather than winning over their proverbial "hearts and minds." As Bacevich noted, "Heavy handed US pacification techniques were inflaming rather than squelching resistance." US forces lashed out, rampaged into homes, arresting, humiliating and torturing Iraqis both within the country, most famously at the infamous Abu Ghraib prison, but also externally through "extraordinary rendition," wherein the Bush administration lawyers sanctioned the creation of a US-led international archipelago of detention and torture centers under new rules of their own making. US detention and sadistic torture replete with leaked photographs and videos proved highly effective recruiting tools for its jihadi adversaries worldwide.

Struggling to recruit a sufficient military force for the GWOT, the US armed forces arbitrarily lengthened commitments and made unprecedented use of mercenary soldiers, some of which flaunted the supposed rules of war by opening fire on civilians and committing other atrocities. In 2006 the Bush administration sent a new "surge" of US forces and claimed to be capitalizing on the "Sunni awakening" in majority Shi'ite Iraq to implement a more effective counterinsurgency (COIN) strategy. The supposed success of "the surge" was little more than another propaganda stunt.

The nation that had refused to learn the lessons of Vietnam had thus created another quagmire for itself in Iraq. Elected in 2008 behind a vow to end the war, which he had voted against authorizing while in the US Senate, Obama declared that US forces would pull out at the end of 2011. Withdrawal turned out to be easier said than done. By that time Iraq had become a magnet for foreign fighters from throughout the Islamic world. A new entity known as *Daesh* (ISIS) sought to create a transnational Islamic caliphate in the region and seized control of some major cities in the process. The United States thus remained mired in Iraq--which remained politically dysfunctional and a humanitarian nightmare—but also stepped up its involvement in Syria to combat *Daesh*. Iran and other Shi'ite forces also opposed and helped defeat *Daesh*, which had received backing from reactionary Sunnis, including Saudi Arabia and other Gulf regimes allied with the United States.

While Obama campaigned against the Iraq War in 2008, he was not an antiwar candidate. He called instead for a revivified US effort against the Taliban, declaring that Afghanistan was "the war we need to win." Obama thus orchestrated a US military surge there, which failed just as completely as the war in Iraq.

The Taliban had built widespread support in the countryside, while in Kabul President Hamid Karzai refused to follow US dictates, which he thought, often with good reason, were ill-informed. Foreign fighters flocked to the cause—especially when photographs circulated of US soldiers burning copies of the Koran or urinating on the bodies of dead Muslims--thus creating a steady supply of enemy jihadis.

The supposed US ally in Pakistan actually did not mind the Taliban, which might prove to be a useful ally or buffer with Pakistan's inveterate enemy, India. The Pakistani military regime readily took billions of dollars from the Americans yet refused or failed to control guerrilla strongholds in the rugged Afghan-Pakistan tribal border region. Finally, the Afghan resistance received ample funding by playing a central role in the world's opium growing and trafficking industry. The Americans and their NATO allies (the alliance having long since made a mockery of being a "North Atlantic" entity) thus flailed away for years in another inconclusive counterinsurgency war, the longest in US history. The United States, which first intervened in Afghanistan to create "another Vietnam" for the Soviet Union, had instead created the reprise of a military quagmire for itself.

Enamored with special operations and especially drone warfare, Obama became the assassination president. He authorized scores of targeted killings, far outpacing his predecessor's drone usage, and even targeting US citizens abroad for summary execution as terrorists.

On this as well as other issues—including increasingly militarized domestic policing—the United States was learning through "security" exchange programs and cross-training with Israel. From the revelations of CIA assassination plots in the mid-1970s until 9/11 the United States had refrained from authorizing assassinations, whereas Israel carried out more targeted killings than any other country in the world. Iranians, including scientists, were a favorite but not the only target of Israeli assassination teams. Under the GWOT, the United States began to follow the lead of the smaller security state and undertook a regular program of assassination by drone attack.

After calling initially for justice for Palestinians, Obama like his predecessors bowed to Israel and its lobby. The United States continued massive funding for Israeli militarism while failing to propel a solution to the Palestine issue, the illegal settlements, and the unilateral occupation of Jerusalem. In 2018 the Trump administration recognized Jerusalem as Israel's capital in direct violation of international law and to the outrage of the Arab-Islamic world. He also recognized the illegal Israeli annexation of the Golan Heights and declined to denounce the government of Benjamin Netanyahu's plans to annex substantial portions of the West Bank.

In 2015 Obama had overcome intense opposition from Israel and the American lobby to successfully negotiate an accord with Iran. The United States lifted international economic sanctions in return for wholly verifiable limits on Iranian uranium enrichment at levels that would preclude developing a nuclear weapon. Israel and the lobby vehemently opposed the accord, which Trump summarily revoked in 2018, thus renewing the perpetual state of belligerence with Iran.

Winterizing the Arab Spring

Erupting in 2011 the "Arab spring" was a hopeful spurt of reform populism that began in Tunisia and spread across the Arab world. The movement was both a threat and an opportunity to imperial America, which exploited it to undermine "rogue" regimes yet at the same time insulated its right-wing allies from the reforms.

The United States seized an opportunity to target Libya, even though it had "commended" Gaddafi for arms control and his belated but genuine cooperation with various anti-terror initiatives. Washington thus once again helped overthrow an Arab dictatorship, spreading disorder while creating its own blowback in the process. As with Iraq, ridding the country of the dictator, which the United States facilitated by providing the Libyan rebels with airpower and logistical support, was the easy part. Amid the ensuing turmoil 11 months after the murder of Gaddafi by a mob in October 2011, Islamic rebels marked the September 11 anniversary by attacking the US compound in Benghazi, killing the American ambassador to Libya and three other officials.

An even more inviting target was the Assad regime in Syria, which the Israelis had long opposed and repeatedly attacked, but which received support from Russia, Iran and Hizbullah. The outside intervention to both rebel and government forces turned Syria into a horrific humanitarian nightmare in which more than 200,000 people were killed as millions of refugees poured out of the country to a largely unwelcoming southern Europe--assuming they could first avoid death at sea.

Another country brutally divided and subjected to proxy wars was Yemen, where in 2015 the Saudis led a coalition of Arab regimes in a military intervention that caused massive death and destruction. The United States backed the reactionary Arab regimes in exaggerating the role of Iran in the Yemeni resistance movement that toppled the longtime dictatorship. Besieged by their oil-rich neighbors, Yemenis suffered tens of thousands of deaths while millions faced famine by 2020.

The Arab spring reform movement thus proved far more destructive than progressive because the most powerful country in the world and its reactionary allies alternately opposed it and exploited it to attack their enemies. The United States thus helped ensure that the absolute monarchies in Saudi Arabia, the UAE, Egypt, Oman, Bahrain and elsewhere suppressed the reform efforts, as did the Iranian regime. The Arab Spring thus became a dark winter.

Throughout the post-World War II era, imperial America had kept the oil flowing, thereby ultimately hastening the onset of the existential global crisis of climate change. Beyond that dubious achievement, the United

160

States had orchestrated decades of militarization and support for the Arab autocracies as well as the Israeli repression of Palestine.

In 2018 Israel formally stamped itself as an apartheid regime, as the Knesset passed the "basic law" affirming that Israel was a "Jewish state," with Hebrew as the official state language, thus relegating the Palestinian minority inside Israel's borders, about a fifth of the population, to a formal second-class citizenship to which they had always been assigned informally. The nation state law undermined the longtime propaganda claim that Israel was the "sole democracy" of the Middle East.

Israel continued its brutal repression of the Gaza Strip, which it subjected to devastating indiscriminate wars in 2009, 2014 and 2021. The Islamic resistance government of Hamas fired rudimentary homemade rockets, which did relatively little damage, in protest over ongoing Israeli oppression and cleansing operations in occupied East Jerusalem. Israel responded with an asymmetrical bloodbath in which it deployed US-funded as well as US-manufactured bombs and Hellfire missiles to pummel the defenseless Strip. The assaults killed and maimed thousands of people, many of them children--and destroyed thousands of homes and businesses. At the same time, Israel and its lobby ensured that neither Congress nor the Obama or Biden administrations interrupted the ferocious assaults, which endured for 51 days in 2014 followed by 11 more days of carnage in 2021.

The Zionist state continued the ceaseless illegal occupation and settlement of the West Bank, as it remained a source of widespread anger helping to fuel Islamic fundamentalism. Reinforcing Israeli aggression, the Israel lobby deployed intimidation and lawfare—including efforts to equate free speech criticism of Israel with anti-Semitism—to combat a global movement of boycott, divestment and sanctions modeled on the resistance to South African apartheid.

US imperialism and war exacted a high price from Americans—literally trillions of dollars were expended—but the humanitarian costs for the people of the Middle East were much greater. "Hundreds of thousands have died excruciating and violent deaths," historian Toby Craig Jones has pointed out. "Poverty, environmental disaster, torture, and wretched living conditions haunt the lives of many in Iraq, Iran, and elsewhere in the region." Meanwhile, the US-backed autocrats, Israeli apartheid, and the American policy of militarized imperialism remained intact.

Chapter 10
Conclusions

On Aug. 29, 2005, Katrina, a Category 4 hurricane, struck the US Gulf Coast, causing widespread damage and destruction from high winds and massive flooding, especially in New Orleans. The storm killed some 1,800 people and was the costliest natural disaster in US history.

What was striking about Hurricane Katrina, in addition to the intensity of the storm, was the delayed and utterly inept federal response to the disaster. Lack of preparedness and mismanagement paralyzed the US response. The storm revealed that the United States, preoccupied with waging its worldwide "war on terror," lacked the capacity to recognize or respond competently to a *domestic* crisis.

George W. Bush, one of the worst presidents in American history, failed in his response to the storm even as he denied climate change and presided over the unwinnable foreign wars that he had initiated. Bush then culminated his disastrous two-term presidency by ushering in the Great Recession, which resulted from deregulation and wanton enabling of out-of-control Wall Street speculation that crashed the US and global economies.

Fifteen years after Hurricane Katrina, Americans chose an even more incompetent and ultimately a much more dangerous president. Like Bush, Donald Trump ensured through tax cuts that a small minority of fabulously wealthy elites got even richer, further cementing the status of the United States as a plutocracy. Despite the tax cuts, the US "defense" budget continued to skyrocket. Contemptuous of scientific rationalism, Trump ignored climate change and refused to take seriously the deadly Covid-19 virus pandemic that broke out in 2020, instead mocking prophylactic steps notably the wearing of masks and social distancing while the nation awaited a vaccine that millions of conspiracy-minded Americans would not accept in any event. Hundreds of thousands of people got sick and died.

Once again, the country that had reacted to 9/11 with such energy and alacrity, albeit in a mindlessly destructive fashion, appeared helpless when faced with a domestic crisis.

Ominously, in his 2020 reelection bid Trump, though a transparently hate-filled and incompetent demagogue, nonetheless received more votes than any other candidate in US history—except for his opponent, former vice president, Joe Biden. Trump and tens of millions of his supporters as well as most Republicans in Congress then sought to undermine the legitimacy of the seamlessly conducted and decisive presidential election.

Trump's resistance--abetted by the toxic cocktail of white nationalism and internet conspiracy theories--ignited the unprecedented violent assault on the US Capitol on Jan. 6, 2021. Right-wing Republicans followed by proposing waves of racist voter suppression legislation in more than half the states. They simultaneously stepped up blatantly undemocratic gerrymandering of congressional districts to maintain their power in Congress. The United States thus faced a domestic political crisis that threatened to spiral out of control.

In the wake of these stunning developments, it has never been clearer that the real threat to "national security" does not emanate from abroad, but rather from political dysfunction and the forces of disintegration within. After decades of promoting militarism and undermining democracy abroad, it was no coincidence that American democracy was falling apart from the inside.

This book has demonstrated that American exceptionalism underlies and ultimately drives the nation's history of waging imperialism and war. It follows logically that the only cure for American foreign policy is to deconstruct and transcend the hegemonic discourse of national self-worship. As the title of this book suggests, the hope for a progressive path forward requires as a first step taking ownership of the long American history of war and imperialism, as opposed to clinging to the self-serving yet ultimately self-destructive chosen-nation narrative. Only by understanding history can we hope to change its course.

Rather than continuing down the destructive path of war and imperialism, the United States thus desperately needs to focus on reforming the "homeland." To be sure, the planet is too interconnected and too interdependent for the United States to adopt a crude Trumpian "America first" platform, characterized by arbitrary trade wars and racist contempt for other peoples of the world. A new paradigm of cooperative internationalism, however, could enable the United States in concert with other nations to address global challenges while carrying out political, economic, and criminal justice reform, among other pressing domestic priorities.

A Vision of Cooperative Internationalism

It is more than obvious, as the crises of climate change and the global pandemic attest, that in this inter-connected world, problem-solving requires global solutions. At present self-serving national patriotism—which Albert Einstein once aptly referenced as "the measles of mankind"--precludes the high level of cooperation that is urgently needed.

The United States must transcend its history of national self-worship, imperialism and militancy and instead join in guiding the world into a new era of cooperative internationalism. Such a vision would entail sweeping arms reduction initiatives and a moratorium on weapons sales; maximum international cooperation on disease prevention and control; commitment to international energy and environmental standards to arrest climate change and end the rampant destruction of animal and plant species and their habitats worldwide; dedicated pursuit of family planning and desperately needed world population control; minimum standards for health and nutrition to prevent famine and reduce the number of refugees and migrants; and toleration of racial, ethnic and religious diversity.

In addition to the above policies, the United States should cut off all financial and political support to countries, including close allies such as Saudi Arabia and Israel, that pursue repressive or racist policies. The United States should stand for international law and invest heavily in human rights, humanitarian reforms, and in the United Nations. Above all, it should lead by the example rather than intervention and do so by addressing domestic needs and striving to preserve and strengthen decency and democracy.

It would of course be more than naïve to expect the United States promptly and willingly to undertake these changes. Millions of Americans are hardly on the brink of replacing their American flags with the banner of the United Nations. The United States remains poised through its archipelago of military bases, its persistent cultivation of enemies, and historical proclivity for war and imperialism to lash out again if provoked—or, as this study has shown, even if not provoked. Sadly, it would be no surprise if new threats were to be manufactured—along the lines of "war by act of Mexico," the Tonkin Gulf incident, or Iraqi weapons of mass destruction—to propel the United States righteously crusading, flags waving, into yet another military conflict.

The unfortunate truth is that it likely will require even more cataclysmic crises than the failed wars, climate-induced disasters, and pandemics we have thus far endured to provoke the much-needed tectonic shift in US foreign policy and in world politics. The forces of racism, reaction, and aggression remain entrenched in American as well as other societies.

164

The unhappy yet inescapable and realistic conclusion of this study is that we, and especially the coming generations, are in for a very rough ride into the global future.

The only way forward for the United States is resolute commitment to progressive reform coupled with an attendant renunciation of self-destructive national militancy. For humanity, and the planet as a whole, there is also only one way forward, and it lies down the path of international cooperation rather than the dead-end course of perpetual nation-state conflict.

www.ingramcontent.com/pod-product-compliance
Lightning Source LLC
Chambersburg PA
CBHW070819100426
42813CB00033B/3439/J